COMPACT
COPYRIGHT

ALA Editions purchases fund advocacy, awareness,
and accreditation programs for library professionals worldwide.

COMPACT
COPYRIGHT

Quick Answers to Common Questions

SARA R. BENSON

ALA
Editions

CHICAGO | 2021

SARA R. BENSON is the copyright librarian and an assistant professor at the University of Illinois Library. She holds a JD from the University of Houston Law Center, an LLM from the University of California at Berkeley, and an MSLIS from the School of Information Science at the University of Illinois. Prior to joining the library, Benson was a lecturer at the University of Illinois College of Law for ten years. She is the host of the podcast ©hat (Copyright Chat), available on iTunes and at https://go.illinois.edu/copyrightchat, and editor of Copyright Conversations: Rights Literacy in a Digital World (ACRL, 2019).

© 2021 by Sara R. Benson

Extensive effort has gone into ensuring the reliability of the information in this book; however, the publisher makes no warranty, express or implied, with respect to the material contained herein.

ISBNs
978-0-8389-3756-3 (paper)
978-0-8389-3803-4 (PDF)
978-0-8389-3802-7 (ePub)

Library of Congress Cataloging-in-Publication Data
Names: Benson, Sara R., author.
Title: Compact copyright : quick answers to common questions / Sara R. Benson.
Description: Chicago : ALA Editions, 2021. | Includes bibliographical references and index. |
    Summary: "This comprehensive guide provides quick answers to frequent copyright questions
    affecting academia, universities, libraries, museums, and archives"—Provided by publisher.
Identifiers: LCCN 2021018218 (print) | LCCN 2021018219 (ebook) | ISBN 9780838937563 (paper-
    back) | ISBN 9780838938034 (pdf) | ISBN 9780838938027 (epub)
Subjects: LCSH: Copyright. | Fair use (Copyright)
Classification: LCC K1420.5 .B45 2021 (print) | LCC K1420.5 (ebook) | DDC 346.7304/82—dc23
LC record available at https://lccn.loc.gov/2021018218
LC ebook record available at https://lccn.loc.gov/2021018219

Cover design by Kim Hudgins. Cover images © Tierney/Adobe Stock.
Text design in the Freight and Fieldwork typefaces by Karen Sheets de Gracia.

♾ This paper meets the requirements of ANSI/NISO Z39.48-1992 (Permanence of Paper).

PRINTED IN THE UNITED STATES OF AMERICA
25 24 23 22 21   5 4 3 2 1

For my greatest loves,
Eric and Avery.

Contents

Preface

This book is like having an at-your-fingertips copyright expert sitting by your side as you engage with copyright issues affecting academia, universities, libraries, museums, and archives. It is an easy-to-read, simply structured guidebook to answering frequent questions that arise in the course of day-to-day work in these settings. It is not a tome of legal theory, a legal treatise full of legalese and policy proposals arguing about what the law should or could be, rather, it is an attempt to make copyright law accessible to individuals working in library and library-adjacent settings.

I will be your copyright guide throughout this book, including excerpts of the law, brief discussions and answers to potential questions you may have. I am an attorney, with both a juris doctor and a master of law, and a librarian, with a master's in library and information science. I teach copyright law to librarians at the University of Illinois School of Information Sciences, where my goal is to make the law accessible to my students; I hope to do the same for the readers of this book. I work as the copyright librarian at the University of Illinois at Urbana–Champaign Library, where I have the pleasure of engaging with copyright on a daily basis.

While you most certainly may wish to read this book from cover to cover, and at some point, it may be valuable to do so, this book can also serve as a ready-made guide for questions at the point of need when you are looking for quick answers to complicated copyright questions. To that end, each chapter of this book is organized in the same way, such that a reader can anticipate how to get to the exact right part of the chapter he or she needs at a given time. Each chapter includes the following sections:

- **THE LAW:** the actual letter of the Copyright Law, including the Copyright Act and key case summaries, where applicable
- **DISCUSSION OF THE LAW:** a discussion of what the law means in practical terms

- **COMMON SCENARIOS:** a few key examples of possible real-life situations involving the law, along with suggested solutions
- **TOOLS & RESOURCES:** a list of helpful articles, websites, and other materials to help you interpret and apply the law

This book is comprehensive, and I have used my experience as a copyright librarian to target common library issues that arise under each section of the law. However, of course, the hypotheticals cannot cover every single scenario you may encounter; or your particular situation may be slightly different. The materials listed in "Tools & Resources" can help you navigate from a mostly on-point hypothetical answer to an answer for your particular situation. Where you still have questions, a more general list in appendix C supplies additional sources of assistance for librarians struggling with copyright questions, or you can post a question to the Copyright Advisory Network forum available at https://library copyright.net/, where you can ask copyright librarians such as myself questions.

This book focuses on United States copyright law. I am an attorney and I have practiced law; however, nothing in this book constitutes legal advice. Librarians in all kinds of libraries—including K–12, academic, public, and private libraries—find themselves making fair use decisions, interpreting rights to make preservation and archival copies, and more. As such, the aim of this book is to help readers make decisions that are more informed and, hopefully, less fraught with stress and uncertainty.

Whether you are reading this book from cover to cover to better familiarize yourself with copyright law generally or going directly to a specific chapter to answer a very particular question in a "just in time" approach, I hope this book empowers you. I hope it empowers you to flex your fair use muscles to create a dazzling library guide or presentation. I hope it empowers you to go further to preserve the materials in your library for posterity. I hope it empowers you to provide greater access to your patrons. Most of all, I hope it furthers the mission of your library through the powerful tools afforded by copyright.

Acknowledgments

No author can stand alone when writing a book, and I am no different. There are so many people and organizations to thank and I'm sure I cannot thank everyone here, so please know that if you are one of my cheerleaders, you are much appreciated.

I do wish to thank a few key people and organizations, though. Of course, first and foremost I must thank my husband, Eric, and my daughter, Avery, for being patient with me as I worked on this book many evenings and weekends and even during early morning gymnastics practice. Without the support of my family, I would be nowhere. I love you both with all my heart. Thank you to my parents and my sisters and my uncle and the rest of my family for loving me unconditionally always. Thank you to my friends who truly are my family by choice for laughing with me, encouraging me, and keeping me going even through long, long bike rides in heavy wind uphill (yes, Laura, I'm talking to you!).

Thank you to the University of Illinois Library and the University of Illinois School of Information Sciences for believing in me and supporting my professional endeavors. I am truly lucky to have wonderful colleagues and a job that gives me so much joy. Thank you to my students at the iSchool for always finding the excitement in copyright law and teaching me something new every semester. A special thank you to Dean John Wilkin for creating my position and for sharing my love of all things copyright.

Thank you to the American Library Association for publishing this book, and especially to Patrick Hogan, senior editor with ALA Publishing, for keeping me on track throughout the writing process. Thank you to Carla Myers for reading early versions of this book and providing me with such thoughtful feedback.

Finally, to all my fellow Copyright Fight Club members (you know who you are): thank you for welcoming me into this profession with arms wide open, allowing me to ask questions and learn from you, and being all-around awesome people. I'm so proud to be one of you and to pay forward your kindness and generosity.

CHAPTER 1

Copyright Basics

THE LAW

United States Constitution, Article I, Section 8, Clause 8: Patent and Copyright Clause

The Congress shall have the power . . . [t]o promote the progress of science and useful arts, by securing for limited times to authors and inventors the exclusive right to their respective writings and discoveries.

United States Copyright Act of 1976, Title 17 of the US Code, Section 102 (2018): Subject Matter of Copyright

(a) Copyright protection subsists, in accordance with this title, in original works of author-ship fixed in any tangible medium of expression, now known or later developed, from which they can be perceived, reproduced, or otherwise communicated, either directly or with the aid of a machine or device. Works of authorship include the following categories:

  (1) literary works;

  (2) musical works, including any accompanying words;

  (3) dramatic works, including any accompanying music;

  (4) pantomimes and choreographic works;

  (5) pictorial, graphic, and sculptural works;

  (6) motion pictures and other audiovisual works;

  (7) sound recordings; and

  (8) architectural works.

(b) In no case does copyright protection for an original work of authorship extend to any idea, procedure, process, system, method of operation, concept, principle, or discovery, regardless of the form in which it is described, explained, illustrated, or embodied in such work.

Title 17, Section 106: Exclusive Rights in Copyrighted Works

Subject to sections 107 through 122, the owner of copyright under this title has the exclusive rights to do and to authorize any of the following:

(1)   to reproduce the copyrighted work in copies or phonorecords;

(2)   to prepare derivative works based upon the copyrighted work;

(3)   to distribute copies or phonorecords of the copyrighted work to the public by sale or other transfer of ownership, or by rental, lease, or lending;

(4)   in the case of literary, musical, dramatic, and choreographic works, pantomimes, and motion pictures and other audiovisual works, to perform the copyrighted work publicly;

(5)   in the case of literary, musical, dramatic, and choreographic works, pantomimes, and pictorial, graphic, or sculptural works, including the individual images of a motion picture or other audiovisual work, to display the copyrighted work publicly; and

(6)   in the case of sound recordings, to perform the copyrighted work publicly by means of a digital audio transmission.

17 U.S Code, Section 201: Ownership of Copyright

(a)   Initial Ownership.—
Copyright in a work protected under this title vests initially in the author or authors of the work. The authors of a joint work are coowners of copyright in the work.

(b)   Works Made for Hire.—
In the case of a work made for hire, the employer or other person for whom the work was prepared is considered the author for purposes of this title, and, unless the parties have expressly agreed otherwise in a written instrument signed by them, owns all of the rights comprised in the copyright.

(c)   Contributions to Collective Works.—
Copyright in each separate contribution to a collective work is distinct from copyright in the collective work as a whole, and vests initially in the author of the contribution. In the absence of an express transfer of the copyright or of any rights under it, the owner of copyright in the collective work is presumed to have acquired only the privilege of reproducing and distributing the contribution as part of that particular collective work, any revision of that collective work, and any later collective work in the same series.

. . .

Title 17, Section 302: Duration of Copyright

(a)   In General.—
Copyright in a work created on or after January 1, 1978, subsists from its creation and, except as provided by the following subsections, endures for a term consisting of the life of the author and 70 years after the author's death.

(b)   Joint Works.—
In the case of a joint work prepared by two or more authors who did not work for hire, the copyright endures for a term consisting of the life of the last surviving author and 70 years after such last surviving author's death.

(c) Anonymous Works and Works Made for Hire.—
In the case of an anonymous work, a pseudonymous work, or a work made for hire, the copyright endures for a term of 95 years from the year of its first publication, or a term of 120 years from the year of its creation, whichever expires first. If, before the end of such term, the identity of one or more of the authors of an anonymous or pseudonymous work is revealed in the records of a registration made for that work under subsections (a) or (d) of section 408, or in the records provided by this subsection, the copyright in the work endures for the term specified by subsection (a) or (b), based on the life of the author or authors whose identity has been revealed. Any person having an interest in the copyright in an anonymous or pseudonymous work may at any time record, in records to be maintained by the Copyright Office for that purpose, a statement identifying one or more authors of the work; the statement shall also identify the person filing it, the nature of that person's interest, the source of the information recorded, and the particular work affected, and shall comply in form and content with requirements that the Register of Copyrights shall prescribe by regulation.

. . .

Key Definitions from Title 17, Section 101

A "collective work" is a work, such as a periodical issue, anthology, or encyclopedia, in which a number of contributions, constituting separate and independent works in themselves, are assembled into a collective whole.

A "compilation" is a work formed by the collection and assembling of preexisting materials or of data that are selected, coordinated, or arranged in such a way that the resulting work as a whole constitutes an original work of authorship. The term "compilation" includes collective works.

A work is "created" when it is fixed in a copy or phonorecord [see below] for the first time; where a work is prepared over a period of time, the portion of it that has been fixed at any particular time constitutes the work as of that time, and where the work has been prepared in different versions, each version constitutes a separate work.

A "derivative work" is a work based upon one or more preexisting works, such as a translation, musical arrangement, dramatization, fictionalization, motion picture version, sound recording, art reproduction, abridgment, condensation, or any other form in which a work may be recast, transformed, or adapted. A work consisting of editorial revisions, annotations, elaborations, or other modifications which, as a whole, represent an original work of authorship, is a "derivative work."

A work is "fixed" in a tangible medium of expression when its embodiment in a copy or phonorecord, by or under the authority of the author, is sufficiently permanent or stable to permit it to be perceived, reproduced, or otherwise communicated for a period of more than transitory duration. A work consisting of sounds, images, or both that are being transmitted is "fixed" for purposes of this title if a fixation of the work is being made simultaneously with its transmission.

"Literary works" are works, other than audiovisual works, expressed in words, numbers, or other verbal or numerical symbols or indicia, regardless of the nature of the material objects, such as books, periodicals, manuscripts, phonorecords, film, tapes, disks, or cards, in which they are embodied.

To "perform" a work means to recite, render, play, dance, or act it, either directly or by means of any device or process or, in the case of a motion picture or other audiovisual work, to show its images in any sequence or to make the sounds accompanying it audible.

"Phonorecords" are material objects in which sounds, other than those accompanying a motion picture or other audiovisual work, are fixed by any method now known or later developed, and from which the sounds can be perceived, reproduced, or otherwise communicated, either directly or with the aid of a machine or device. The term "phonorecords" includes the material object in which the sounds are first fixed.

"Pictorial, graphic, and sculptural works" include two-dimensional and three-dimensional works of fine, graphic, and applied art, photographs, prints and art reproductions, maps, globes, charts, diagrams, models, and technical drawings, including architectural plans. Such works shall include works of artistic craftsmanship insofar as their form but not their mechanical or utilitarian aspects are concerned; the design of a useful article, as defined in this section, shall be considered a pictorial, graphic, or sculptural work only if, and only to the extent that, such design incorporates pictorial, graphic, or sculptural features that can be identified separately from, and are capable of existing independently of, the utilitarian aspects of the article.

"Sound recordings" are works that result from the fixation of a series of musical, spoken, or other sounds, but not including the sounds accompanying a motion picture or other audiovisual work, regardless of the nature of the material objects, such as disks, tapes, or other phonorecords, in which they are embodied.

A "work made for hire" is—

(1) a work prepared by an employee within the scope of his or her employment; or

(2) a work specially ordered or commissioned for use as a contribution to a collective work, as a part of a motion picture or other audiovisual work, as a translation, as a supplementary work, as a compilation, as an instructional text, as a test, as answer material for a test, or as an atlas, if the parties expressly agree in a written instrument signed by them that the work shall be considered a work made for hire.

DISCUSSION OF THE LAW

In conducting copyright workshops over the years, I have learned that many people overestimate the amount of work entailed to own a copyright. In my experience, most people think that there is some special action one must take to own a copyright, such as affixing the work with a copyright notice or registering the work with the copyright office. Although at one time those kinds of copyright formalities were a part of U.S. law, that is no longer true. There is no special language that one must use, and no special notification that needs to take place in order to own a copyright. In fact, many people own multiple copyrights.

Works Covered

So, if no special action must be taken to own a copyright, what kinds of works qualify for copyright protection under U.S. law? The first thing to know is that copyright is about creativity. In fact, Congress was granted the power to create the Copyright Act in the U.S. Constitution. Article I, Section 8, Clause 8 provides that "Congress shall have the power . . . [t]o promote the progress of science . . . by securing for limited times to authors . . . the exclusive right to their respective writings." Copyright law is a particular kind of intellectual property law and, rather than protecting a specific physical output, it is aimed at protecting the author's creativity in coming up with the unique expression involved in that creative output. Copyright law protects innovative creativity in the areas of writing, music, movies, creative arts, and more. As noted in Section 102 of the Copyright Act, copyright protects the rights of authors of literary works, musical works and sound recordings, dramatic works, graphical works, and more. Copyright law even views computer code as a type of literary work and, as such, protects the work of authors in writing code language as well. For most librarians, the types of work most likely to be of interest are the kinds of works housed in libraries: written literary works and music. However, as libraries expand to include more and different kinds of works, librarians will often find themselves learning about the intricacies of copyright law as it relates to computer code, computer software, and more.

It is often easier to define the scope of copyright by looking at what it does not protect. Section 102 notes that copyright law does not protect ideas or concepts, including facts; nor does it cover anything that could be patentable such as a "procedure, process, system, method of operation, concept, principle, or discovery." Similarly, there is a distinction between copyright and trademark in that copyright does not protect titles and short phrases such as "Just do it," which may otherwise be the mark of a business, such as Nike, and protected under trademark. Although copyright does not protect facts or data alone, it does provide a "thin layer" of copyright protection for the arrangement or compilation of facts.[1]

If a work is something that is copyrightable, what are the requirements for a copyright to attach to a particular work? There are only two: first, the work must be of a sufficient minimal level of originality or creativity; and second, the work must be fixed (that is, written down or recorded) in a tangible medium (in a computer, on a piece of paper, or the like). The bar is rather low—one need not be a Picasso to obtain a copyright. Generally, a copyright will attach if the author has made creative choices sufficient to justify the determination that the work is original. For instance, for a work of photography, the author has chosen to take a photo at a specific angle with specific lighting of a particular subject at a particular point in time.[2] And, in terms of originality, the Supreme Court has said that "original, as the term is used in copyright, means only that the work was independently created by the author (as opposed to copied from other works), and that it possesses at least some minimal degree of creativity."[3] The Supreme Court has further noted that "the requisite level of creativity is extremely low; even a slight amount will suffice."[4]

Ownership

If something is copyrightable, the owner of the work is the author, at least unless and until the copyright is transferred in writing to another owner.[5] The author is the person who created the work. If multiple authors joined efforts to create the work and intended that the work be combined, then the work will be jointly owned by all the authors. In that case, each of the authors has the right to license the work, but the authors must split any profits. These default copyright rules can, of course, be modified by a contractual agreement between the authors. Another wrinkle in the ownership rules occurs when a work is made by an employee within the scope of employment. In that instance, the work is actually owned by the employer and not the employee, under the "work made for hire" doctrine. Today, a work may also be considered a work made for hire if it falls within a specific list of types of works, including a contribution to a collected work, a translation, a test, and the like, so long as the "parties expressly agree in a written instrument signed by them that the work shall be considered a work made for hire."[6] A work made for hire has a different copyright length and is not subject to termination rights, so whether a particular work constitutes a work made for hire should be considered routinely when making copyright determinations. One should also note that in many academic institutions, academic and scholarly works created by professors would normally be considered a work made for hire but are often "gifted" back to the author by university policy.[7] Finally, the definition of a work made for hire has changed over time. For works copyrighted under the 1909 act, which remained in effect until January 1, 1978, the act did not define work made for hire; but courts interpreted it as including works created by salaried employees as well as, in the case of independent contractors, whether the work was created at the "instance and expense" of the employer.[8]

The author or authors own the exclusive copyright to their works unless and until they grant licenses or permissions to others. The rights that the author owns are often referred to as a "bundle of rights" and include the right to reproduce the work; distribute it; perform it; display it; and create derivative works. Most of these rights are as straightforward as they sound—for instance, the right to reproduce the work is the right to make copies of the work. The right to create derivative works is probably the most confusing right, as many people are not quite sure how "much" addition to the work would constitute a derivative work or where the line is between a derivative work, which would constitute an infringement, and a transformative work, which would constitute a fair use of the original work. First, the Copyright Act provides a definition for a derivative work: "A work based upon one or more preexisting works, such as a translation, musical arrangement, dramatization, fictionalization, motion picture version, sound recording, art reproduction, abridgment, condensation, or any other form in which a work may be recast, transformed, or adapted. A work consisting of editorial revisions, annotations, elaborations, or other modifications which, as a whole, represent an original work of authorship, is a 'derivative work'."[9] Second, fan fiction is a prime example of work that could constitute either an impermissible derivative work or a permissible fair use depending on the work (see a case study about this topic in chapter 10, "Fair Use"). Third, there are many exceptions to copyright, so even though these are the exclusive rights of the copyright owner, exceptions may apply.

The rules regarding the length of copyright have changed over time and these rules are generally not retroactive. That means that the rules for copyright in the U.S. were different in 1930 than they are today. Today, copyrights last for the length of the author's life plus an additional seventy years after their death. With joint authors, the copyright will not expire until seventy years after the death of the longest-surviving author. Copyrights always expire at the end of the calendar year as well. The rule is a bit different for works made for hire, which last for 120 years from the date of creation.

Copyright Notice

Although a work no longer needs a copyright notice to have a valid copyright, it is still advisable to include a copyright notice on an original work. Providing such a notice makes others aware of the copyright status of the work and eliminates the "innocent infringer" defense.[10] In other words, it creates a rebuttable presumption in court that the person violating the copyright was aware that it was a copyrighted work. It is also advisable to register the work with the copyright office in a timely fashion. You cannot sue a copyright infringer unless you have registered the work, and a timely registration of the work preserves your right to obtain high statutory damages for violations of the copyright.

COMMON SCENARIOS

⊃ **A graduate student contacts you to ask who owns the written work completed for a portion of their thesis. The student notes that their advisor assisted with the research for the work as well as writing the work, but has since told the student that this work cannot be used for a portion of the thesis because the professor is now submitting it for publication as a sole-authored work.**

The very first thing I tell anyone on campus when they ask me a question like this is that I am a librarian, not their lawyer, and that if they need legal advice, they should seek advice from an attorney.

If they still want to know what information exists to answer this question, I would start to look for some helpful documents. The first thing at play when there are professors and students writing creative output is the "work made for hire" doctrine. The default rule for work produced by employees in the scope of their employment (the professor, at least) is that the university would own the work. Of course, this default rule is often overwritten by university statutes and general rules. At the University of Illinois, for instance, the university statutes provide that students and faculty own their own work.

Starting from the assumption that the copyrights involved in writing a thesis would be owned by the student, the general rules for joint works should be considered. If the student and professor combined efforts and intended for the work to be a joint work, then they both own the work equally. It is important, of course, to ask whether there were any written agreements to the contrary, as these general rules can always be modified by contract. If not, however, the student should be assured that the work is jointly owned and, as such, the professor cannot tell the student not to use the work. In these kinds of situations, however, more is often at play than just copyright. The student, for instance, may need the professor's support for their career. In this scenario, besides pointing out the copyright rules to the student, a referral to the graduate college for further advice is likely warranted.

⤳ **A librarian contacts you for advice regarding the copyright status of some letters written by a union organizer in the 1930s who died in 1947. Are the letters in the public domain?**

This question is typical in that it seems fairly straightforward, but actually is quite complicated when fully addressed. Assuming the letters were unpublished when they were written, the default rule for unpublished works created in the United States is that the copyright expired seventy years after the death of the author, or "works from authors who died before 1949." Whether the letters are considered a work made for hire depends on the context in which they were made. For example, the letters may have been written by the union organizer in an official capacity. If so, the letters would constitute a work made for hire and would have a different copyright length. If the letters constitute a work made for hire, the copyright would extend to 120 years from the date of creation. The determination of whether a specific item was a work made for hire can constitute a factual analysis and should be made by looking at the specific letters, the timing of when they were made (during working hours?), and multiple other factors. Thus, the librarian would be encouraged to consult circular 30, *Works Made for Hire*, from the U.S. Copyright Office, as well as to consider the context in which the specific letters were made to make the best determination about whether they should be considered works made for hire.

⤳ **A graduate student writing a dissertation contacts you to ask whether she can include a portion of her work that she previously included in a journal publication as a chapter in her dissertation. Can she?**

The answer, as with many situations in copyright—is it depends. While the graduate student originally owned the copyright to the entire work, when she entered into a publishing agreement with the journal, she may have transferred her copyright to the journal through the publishing agreement. However, she may have retained some rights (such as to use the work in a dissertation), or she may have retained all her rights if she was required only to transfer a nonexclusive license to the journal for publication. It is important, then, for the student to read the author agreement she signed with the journal. If she no longer has the agreement, she can check the journal website (they often include copyright information for prospective authors) or contact the journal directly. This is a teachable moment for the student, though, and should not go to waste. Encouraging the student to negotiate author's agreements with journal publishers is a good way to avoid these kinds of issues in the future (for instance, if she wishes to use her publication for teaching, to create derivative works, or to present at conferences). See also the "Tools & Resources" section in this chapter for SPARC's brochure on author agreements and the Author's Alliance tool for negotiating agreements.

TOOLS & RESOURCES

UNITED STATES COPYRIGHT OFFICE

The U.S. Copyright Office produces several useful resources on copyright, and their website (www.copyright.gov) is great to reference when trying to explain copyright or learn more about it.

Compendium of U.S. Copyright Office Practices, **3rd ed.** Washington, D.C.: U.S. Copyright Office, 2021. https://www.copyright.gov/comp3/.

> Another tool that will be useful to all issues relating to United States copyright is the *Copyright Compendium*. Now in its third edition, the *Compendium* is a thorough guide to the Copyright Office's practices and explains many common issues.

Copyright Basics. Circular 1, 2019. https://www.copyright.gov/circs/circ01.pdf.

> This succinct, helpful guide from the Copyright Office provides readers with the copyright basics.

Works Made for Hire. Circular 30, 2017. https://www.copyright.gov/circs/circ30.pdf.

> This guide explains the concept of work made for hire under the 1976 version of the Copyright Act. (For pre-1976 works, covered by the 1909 Copyright Act, see https://www.copyright.gov/comp3/chap2100/doc/appendixE-madeforhire.pdf.)

Works Not Protected by Copyright. Circular 33, 2017. https://www.copyright.gov/circs/circ33.pdf.

> This guide shares information about what is not constituted as a copyrightable work.

UNITED STATES PATENT AND TRADEMARK OFFICE (USPTO)

"Copyright Basics." https://www.uspto.gov/ip-policy/copyright-policy/copyright-basics.

> The USPTO has resources that serve as an excellent introduction to copyright.

Global Intellectual Property Academy. "Overview of Copyrights."
http://www.uspto.gov/video/cbt/GIPA-English/copyright/index.htm.

If you prefer to watch a presentation about copyright basics, this accurate presentation is handy. A transcript is included.

ADDITIONAL RESOURCES ON COPYRIGHT

Hirtle, Peter. "Copyright Term and the Public Domain in the United States." Cornell Copyright Information Center, 2020. https://copyright.cornell.edu/publicdomain.

This chart will prove useful throughout this book and will be included often as a resource. It can be used as a quick reference to understand the way U.S. copyright law has changed over time.

Schofield, Brianna L., and Robert Kirk Walker, eds. *Understanding and Negotiating Book Publication Contracts.* Author's Alliance, 2018. https://www.authorsalliance.org/wp-content/uploads/2018/10/20181003_AuthorsAllianceGuidePublicationContracts.pdf.

This guide is a very helpful tool for those negotiating monograph agreements.

The Scholarly Publishing and Academic Resources Coalition (SPARC). "Author Rights: Using the SPARC Author Addendum." https://sparcopen.org/our-work/author-rights/brochure-html/.

A nice, succinct addendum that can be added to author's agreements.

NOTES

1. *Feist Publications, Inc. v. Rural Telephone Serv. Co.*, 499 U.S. 340 (1991).
2. See *Burrow-Giles Lithographic Co. v. Sarony*, 111 U.S. 53 (1884).
3. *Feist, supra*, 499 U.S. at 345.
4. *Id.*
5. Note that the transfer of the exclusive rights to copyright must be made in signed writing. 17 U.S.C. § 204(a) (2018). However, nonexclusive licenses or transfers of copyright may be made orally.
6. 17 U.S.C. § 101.
7. Sara R. Benson, "'I Own It, Don't I?' The Rules of Academic Copyright Ownership and You," *College and Undergraduate Libraries* 26, no. 4 (2018): 317–27.
8. U.S. Copyright Office, *"Work Made for Hire" under the 1909 Copyright Law* (leaflet, 2005), https://www.copyright.gov/comp3/chap2100/doc/appendixE-madeforhire.pdf.

9. 17 U.S.C. § 101.

10. U.S. Copyright Office, "Chapter 4: Copyright Notice, Deposit, and Registration, 405(b)," in *Copyright Law of the United States (Title 17)* (2021), https://www.copyright.gov/title17/92chap4.html#405.

CHAPTER 2

The First Sale Doctrine

Title 17, Section 109: Limitations on Exclusive Rights—Effect of Transfer of a Particular Copy or Phonorecord

(a) Notwithstanding the [author's exclusive right to distribution], the owner of a particular copy or phonorecord lawfully made under this title, or any person authorized by such owner, is entitled, without the authority of the copyright owner, to sell or otherwise dispose of the possession of that copy or phonorecord. . . .

(b)(1)(A) Notwithstanding the provisions of subsection (a), unless authorized by the owners of copyright in the sound recording . . . neither the owner of a particular phonorecord nor any person in possession of a particular copy of a computer program (including any tape, disk, or other medium embodying such program), may, for the purposes of direct or indirect commercial advantage, dispose of, or authorize the disposal of, the possession of that phonorecord or computer program (including any tape, disk, or other medium embodying such program) by rental, lease, or lending, or by any other act or practice in the nature of rental, lease, or lending. Nothing in the preceding sentence shall apply to the rental, lease, or lending of a phonorecord for nonprofit purposes by a nonprofit library or nonprofit educational institution. The transfer of possession of a lawfully made copy of a computer program by a nonprofit educational institution to another nonprofit educational institution or to faculty, staff, and students does not constitute rental, lease, or lending for direct or indirect commercial purposes under this subsection.

. . .

(b)(2)(B) Nothing in this subsection shall apply to the lending of a computer program for nonprofit purposes by a nonprofit library, if each copy of a computer program which is lent by such library has affixed to the packaging containing the program a warning of copyright in accordance with requirements that the Register of Copyrights shall prescribe by regulation.

. . .

(c) Notwithstanding the [author's exclusive right of public display] the owner of a particular copy lawfully made under this title, or any person authorized by such owner, is entitled, without the authority of the copyright owner, to display that copy publicly, either directly or by the projection of no more than one image at a time, to viewers present at the place where the copy is located.

(d) The privileges prescribed by subsections (a) and (c) do not, unless authorized by the copyright owner, extend to any person who has acquired possession of the copy or phonorecord from the copyright owner, by rental, lease, loan, or otherwise, without acquiring ownership of it.

. . .

DISCUSSION OF THE LAW

Most library lending operates under the first sale doctrine (also known as the exhaustion doctrine). At its most basic, the first sale doctrine states that the distribution right of the copyright owner expires after they have sold the physical copy of the work. It is important to note that the sale of the work triggers the first sale doctrine and that simply licensing a work does not.[1] It is also important to note that the first sale doctrine allows the distribution of the book that was purchased, not a copy of the book. In other words, the first sale doctrine does not permit a library to make multiple copies of a book and distribute the copies. Rather, it permits the library to lend the book that was purchased. Once the original copyright owner has sold the book once, the owner of the book (or other item) is able to sell the book, rent the book to another person, lend the book to another person, or otherwise dispose of the book in any way. This doctrine explains why public and academic libraries can lend the physical books that they purchase as many times as they wish without paying an extra fee (and so can individuals in little free libraries in their front yards, for instance). It also explains why libraries can sell old or used books and recoup those expenses without worrying about providing any remuneration to the book publisher. For instance, the Supreme Court case allowed a student from Thailand to purchase textbooks at a cheaper price, sell them in the United States, and keep the profits.[2]

This doctrine does not permit individuals to lend or lease computer programs or sound recordings for a fee. However, libraries and educational institutions may still lend computer programs and sound recordings but must affix a copyright warning notice to the packaging.

The first sale doctrine, Section 109 of the Copyright Act, also permits the owner of a lawful copy of a work to display the work publicly either "directly" (such as in an exhibit box) or "by the projection of no more than one image at a time, to viewers present at the place where the copy is located." Note that this does not apply to someone who does not own the work but is merely renting it. "To cite a familiar example, a person who has rented a print of a motion picture from the copyright owner would have no right to rent it to someone else without the owner's permission."[3] Thus, one could project an image in a presentation to those inside the library where the work is housed. But, for instance, in order to put the work in a digital display that would be projected to a larger audience through the internet, the first sale doctrine would not apply. That does not mean the digital display would necessarily violate copyright; however, it may require a fair use analysis (see chapter 10, "Fair Use").

COMMON SCENARIOS

⊃ **A graduate assistant just started working in your library in the interlibrary loan department. He receives a request to loan an entire book that is still in copyright to a library fifty miles away. He is considering shipping the book to the library, but he is worried about violating copyright. Can the graduate assistant ship the physical book to the other library without violating copyright?**

Yes. The first sale doctrine applies and the publisher receives no further remuneration for the lending of the library book after the library owns a copy of the book. Of course, this scenario would change greatly if the graduate assistant, instead of shipping the book, wishes to photocopy the entire book and send the photocopy of the book to the other library. Section 108 of the Copyright Act may permit the interlibrary loan of an entire photocopy of a book, but only in quite limited circumstances. (For more on Section 108, see chapter 5, "Interlibrary Loan and Unsupervised Patron Copying.") Generally, the answer to the question whether a graduate assistant can photocopy an entire book and send it through interlibrary loan is no.

⊃ **A graduate assistant is planning an exhibit in the library archives on the third floor. As part of the exhibit, she wishes to display unique, very old, but still in-copyright letters from a famous author that the library has in its archival collection. She also wishes to use a slide display projected on the wall in the lobby of the library to let patrons know about the exhibit on the third floor. Can she exhibit the letter? Can she project a photo of the letter onto the wall in the lobby to let patrons know about the exhibit?**

Yes, and yes. Section 109 of the Copyright Act explicitly allows the owner of a lawful copy of a work to display that copy publicly without permission of the copyright owner—so long as the people viewing the work are physically present at the location of the copy. That same section of the Copyright Act also permits a limited projection (one image at a time) of a lawfully owned copy of a copyrighted work.

⊃ **The head of the music library has a collection of old but still in-copyright music CDs. Many of them are duplicates, others are simply being weeded from the collection. The head wishes to sell the CDs in a used CD sale to the public to raise funds for the library. Can they?**

Yes. Much as the right of first sale permits owners of lawful CDs to sell them on eBay, the head of the library can sell the CDs to the public. There may be other rules governing the sale, such as procurement rules, but copyright law does not prevent the sale of the physical CDs.

TOOLS & RESOURCES

American Library Association. "Copyright for Libraries: First Sale Doctrine." Last updated March 21, 2019. https://libguides.ala.org/copyright/firstsale.

A helpful library guide from the American Library Association that explains the first sale doctrine.

House Report No. 94-1476. Available from https://www.law.cornell.edu/uscode/text/17/109 in the Notes tab.

The first sale doctrine is further explained in the notes accompanying the statute, which are freely available online.

NOTES

1. *Adobe Systems, Inc. v. One Stop Micro, Inc.*, 84 F. Supp. 2d 1086 (N.D. Cal. 2000).
2. *Kirtsaeng v. Wiley & Sons, Inc.*, 568 U.S. 519 (2013).
3. House Report No. 94-1476, available from https://www.law.cornell.edu/uscode/text/17/109. (Click on the Notes tab on this web page to view the House Report.)

CHAPTER 3

The Public Domain

United States Constitution, Article I, Section 8, Clause 8

The Congress shall have the power . . . [t]o promote the progress of science . . ., by securing for limited times to authors . . . the exclusive right to their respective writings.

Title 17, Section 105: Subject Matter of Copyright

Copyright protection under this title is not available for any work of the United States Government, but the United States Government is not precluded from receiving and holding copyrights transferred to it by assignment, bequest, or otherwise.

Title 17, Section 108(h)–(i): Limitations on Exclusive Rights—Reproductions by Libraries and Archives

(h)

(1) For purposes of this section, during the last 20 years of any term of copyright of a published work, a library or archives, including a nonprofit educational institution that functions as such, may reproduce, distribute, display, or perform in facsimile or digital form a copy or phonorecord of such work, or portions thereof, for purposes of preservation, scholarship, or research, if such library or archives has first determined, on the basis of a reasonable investigation, that none of the conditions set forth in subparagraphs (A), (B), and (C) of paragraph (2) apply.

(2) No reproduction, distribution, display, or performance is authorized under this subsection if—

(A) the work is subject to normal commercial exploitation;

(B) a copy or phonorecord of the work can be obtained at a reasonable price; or

(C) the copyright owner or its agent provides notice pursuant to regulations promulgated by the Register of Copyrights that either of the conditions set forth in subparagraphs (A) and (B) applies.

(3) The exemption provided in this subsection does not apply to any subsequent uses by users other than such library or archives.

(i)   The rights of reproduction and distribution under this section do not apply to a musical work, a pictorial, graphic or sculptural work, or a motion picture or other audiovisual work other than an audiovisual work dealing with news, except that no such limitation shall apply with respect to rights granted by subsections (b), (c), and (h) [.]

Title 17, Section 302 (c)–(e): Duration of Copyright

(c)   Anonymous Works, Pseudonymous Works, and Works Made for Hire.—
In the case of an anonymous work, a pseudonymous work, or a work made for hire, the copyright endures for a term of 95 years from the year of its first publication, or a term of 120 years from the year of its creation, whichever expires first. If, before the end of such term, the identity of one or more of the authors of an anonymous or pseudonymous work is revealed in the records of a registration made for that work . . . , or in the records provided by this subsection, the copyright in the work endures for the term [for an author, life of the author plus 70 years, or for the term of joint authors], based on the life of the author or authors whose identity has been revealed. Any person having an interest in the copyright in an anonymous or pseudonymous work may at any time record, in records to be maintained by the Copyright Office for that purpose, a statement identifying one or more authors of the work; the statement shall also identify the person filing it, the nature of that person's interest, the source of the information recorded, and the particular work affected, and shall comply in form and content with requirements that the Register of Copyrights shall prescribe by regulation.

(d)   Records Relating to Death of Authors.—
Any person having an interest in a copyright may at any time record in the Copyright Office a statement of the date of death of the author of the copyrighted work, or a statement that the author is still living on a particular date. The statement shall identify the person filing it, the nature of that person's interest, and the source of the information recorded, and shall comply in form and content with requirements that the Register of Copyrights shall prescribe by regulation. The Register shall maintain current records of information relating to the death of authors of copyrighted works, based on such recorded statements and, to the extent the Register considers practicable, on data contained in any of the records of the Copyright Office or in other reference sources.

(e)   Presumption as to Author's Death.—
After a period of 95 years from the year of first publication of a work, or a period of 120 years from the year of its creation, whichever expires first, any person who obtains from the Copyright Office a certified report that the records provided by subsection (d) disclose nothing to indicate that the author of the work is living, or died less than 70 years before, is entitled to the benefits of a presumption that the author has been dead for at least 70 years. Reliance in good faith upon this presumption shall be a complete defense to any action for infringement under this title.

Title 17, Section 405: Notice of Copyright—Omission of Notice on Certain Copies and Phonorecords

(c) Effect of Omission on Copyright.—

With respect to copies and phonorecords publicly distributed by authority of the copyright owner before the effective date of the Berne Convention Implementation Act of 1988, the omission of the copyright notice described in sections 401 through 403 from copies or phonorecords publicly distributed by authority of the copyright owner does not invalidate the copyright in a work if—

(1) the notice has been omitted from no more than a relatively small number of copies or phonorecords distributed to the public; or

(2) registration for the work has been made before or is made within five years after the publication without notice, and a reasonable effort is made to add notice to all copies or phonorecords that are distributed to the public in the United States after the omission has been discovered; or

(3) the notice has been omitted in violation of an express requirement in writing that, as a condition of the copyright owner's authorization of the public distribution of copies or phonorecords, they bear the prescribed notice.

Title 17, Section 1401(f): Unauthorized Use of Pre-1972 Sound Recordings

(f) Limitations on Remedies.

(1) Fair use; uses by libraries, archives, and educational institutions.

(A) In general. The limitations on the exclusive rights of a copyright owner described in sections 107, 108, 109, 110, and 112(f) shall apply to a claim under subsection (a) with respect to a sound recording fixed before February 15, 1972.

(B) Rule of construction for section 108(h). With respect to the application of section 108(h) to a claim under subsection (a) with respect to a sound recording fixed before February 15, 1972, the phrase "during the last 20 years of any term of copyright of a published work" in such section 108(h) shall be construed to mean at any time after the date of enactment of this section.

DISCUSSION OF THE LAW

The United States Copyright Office notes "A work of authorship is in the 'public domain' if it is no longer under copyright protection or if it failed to meet the requirements for copyright protection. Works in the public domain may be used freely without the permission of the former copyright owner."[1] Thus works that are quite old, such as Shakespearean works, are in the public domain because the term of copyright protection has expired. If the rightsholder wishes, they can donate works to the public domain by using a license aimed at communicating to the public that the author does not wish to protect the work, such as a Creative Commons Zero (CC0) mark. There are a few different kinds of public domain works discussed in this section, so they are broken down into distinct types, including:

- government works
- works first published in the United States between 1924 and 1978
- works published in the United States with failed formalities between 1924 and 1978
- works published without notice and without registration between 1978 and March 1, 1989
- unpublished works
- works donated to the public domain through open licensing
- pseudo public domain works (for libraries), such as:
  - works in the last twenty years of copyright protection (for use by libraries)
  - pre-1972 sound recordings under the Music Modernization Act (for use by libraries)

Government Works

Under Section 105 of the Copyright Act, "a work prepared by an officer or employee of the United States Government as part of that person's official duties" (e.g., statutes and regulations) are not eligible for copyright protection. Although this appears to be a fairly straightforward rule, there are instances where works published by the United States government are deemed high security or private, and while these works are in the public domain, they are not made available to the public.[2] There are limited exceptions to this rule, including an exception allowing civilian members of certain military institutions to own the copyright to their work while providing the government with an irrevocable, nonexclusive license to the work.[3]

Generally, under the "government edicts doctrine," state and federal laws, including case law, are in the public domain.[4] However, when case law annotations are included with public domain statutes, there has been a dispute as to whether those annotations could be copyrighted. The Supreme Court has ultimately concluded that those case annotations included with the official code "are ineligible for copyright protection" because that author—the legislature—like judges, cannot be the "author" as such, according to the government edicts doctrine.[5]

It is also important to note that this rule is applicable to the federal government. State governments and state laws vary as to how "open" government documents are, beyond case law and official statutes.

Works Published in the United States between 1925 and 1978

Copyright law in the United States has been far from stagnant. It has been reformed many times, including in 1831, 1909, 1962, and 1976. All these changes make it difficult to apply duration terms because these terms have been, over time, a moving target. For instance, the original term for copyright protection was just fourteen years, with a possible renewal term of an additional fourteen years, whereas today the copyright term is life of the author plus seventy years. Figure 3.1 will help you visualize what a moving target duration terms have been.

The date when materials published in the United States enter the public domain is significant, and there are several important factors to note about this date. First, there was a twenty-year gap in the public domain due to the

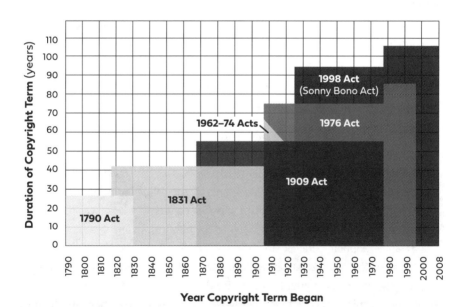

FIGURE 3.1 Trend of Maximum U.S. General Copyright Term

Image has been adapted from Tom W. Bell, *Trend of Maximum U.S. General Copyright Term* (July 23, 2008). CC BY-SA 3.0.

enactment of the Sonny Bono Copyright Term Extension Act (CTEA) in 1998. That act, driven largely by Disney to protect Mickey Mouse, added an extra twenty years of copyright protection to works that would have otherwise entered the public domain starting in 1998. When that act was proposed, the set copyright protection length was seventy-five years from date of publication. However, the CTEA extended the copyright term of future works from life of the author plus fifty years to life of the author plus seventy years; and works that might otherwise enter into the public domain at that time also received an additional twenty years of copyright protection (i.e., date of publication plus ninety-five years instead of seventy-five years). Hence, the public domain faced a gap of twenty years between 1998 and 2018, when no published works from the United States entered into the public domain due to a lapse of copyright.

Second, this date is a moving target. Works first began to enter into the public domain on January 1, 2019, because copyright from works published in 1923 in the United States had expired (1923 + 95 = 2018, and copyright always expires at the end of the calendar year according to the Copyright Act).[6] On January 1, 2020, works published in the United States in 1924 entered the public domain, and so on, until we reach more-modern-era works with the new copyright term length of life of the author plus seventy years (which applied starting in 1978).

Works Published in the United States with Failed Formalities between 1925 and 1978

From the era between 1925 and 1978, some works will enter the public domain for failure to comply with copyright formalities. In that era, a work was required to include a copyright notice in order to receive copyright protection. The notice was required to be placed on the title page or the following page of the work and was required to be structured in a specific manner. If a work was published without a copyright notice, then it fell into the public domain.

Despite popular belief, copyright registration has never been a requirement for securing copyright protection. However, if a copyright owner did not register and renew a copyright notice with the Copyright Office, then the copyright would expire after the first copyright term. Thus, in order to claim the full length of copyright protection (or ninety-five years) in the era between 1924 and 1978, a copyright claimant had to correctly include a copyright notice on the title page (or the page immediately following it) of the work, register the work with the Copyright Office, and renew the copyright with the copyright office. If the renewal was not filed in the work's twenty-eighth year, the copyright expired after the first term of twenty-eight years.

Works Published without Notice and without Registration between 1978 and March 1, 1989

Notice was still required in this era of copyright law, but was not necessarily required on the title page or the page immediately following. In that era, the copyright notice needed to be placed "in such a manner and location as to give reasonable notice of the claim of copyright."[7] In this era of publication, if a work did not have a proper copyright notice but was registered with the Copyright Office within five years after the publication of the work, the work would still be granted copyright protection for the full term—the life of the author plus seventy years for a work published by an individual; or, for a corporate work, either ninety-five years from publication of the work or one hundred and twenty years from creation, whichever expired first.[8] Thus a work would enter the public domain if it was published between 1978 and March 1, 1989, was published without notice, and was not registered with the Copyright Office within five years after publication.

Unpublished Works

The Copyright Act defines a publication as "the distribution of copies of a work to the public by sale [or lease] . . . or offering to distribute copies of a work . . . to a group of persons for purposes of further distribution, public performance or public display."[9] The act further notes that a "public performance or display of a work does not of itself constitute publication."[10] Hence, if a work is not sold, leased, or distributed widely, it is not considered published under the Copyright Act. For works created prior to 1976, publication is not defined in the act, but the 1909 act notes that publication occurs "when copies of the first authorized edition were placed on sale, sold, or publicly distributed by the proprietor of the copyright or under his authority."[11] Case law interpreting the 1909 act has noted that public performance alone is not enough to constitute publication, nor was a limited publication enough to constitute publication.[12] Limited publication occurs when the work is offered to a small amount of people with a limitation on their further distribution of the work (e.g., the rightsholder asks that it not be further transmitted to others).[13] Although I have attempted to clarify how to determine whether a work was published or unpublished for copyright purposes, it is often difficult, and reasonable judges disagree. To that end, the United States Copyright Office issued a notice of inquiry on December 4, 2019, regarding "online publication," asking for "the perspectives and suggestions of copyright owners and the general public regarding possible new regulations interpreting the statutory definition of publication for registration purposes and policy guidance regarding the role that publication should play in copyright law and the registration process."[14] This process is ongoing, but you can also find useful information for determining publication status in the Copyright Office's *Compendium*.[15]

If a work is unpublished under copyright law, then it enters into the public domain seventy years after the death of the author, when the author is known. Thus, in 2020, unpublished works created by authors who died before 1950 are in the public domain. In 2021, that date will be 1951, in 2022 the date will be 1952, and so on.

If the author of an unpublished work is unknown, the work is anonymous, or the work is a work made for hire, then the copyright expires 120 years after the date of creation. Generally, for those types of unpublished works, if the work was created before 1900, it is in the public domain in 2020 (1901 in 2021, and so on). Note that the person attempting to use an anonymous work can contact the United States Copyright Office to get certification that the author is not living (after the 120-year term from the date of creation has expired). Such a certification from the Copyright Office constitutes a presumption that the author is no longer living and is a complete defense to copyright infringement.

Works Donated to the Public Domain through Open Licensing

Many works are in the public domain because they were donated to it by the author. An author creating a work today can choose to use an open license—such as a Creative Commons Zero, or CC0, license—on the work to indicate to the public that the work is in the public domain.

Pseudo–Public Domain Works (for Use by Libraries and Archives)

Published Works in the Last Twenty Years of Copyright Protection

When the 1998 CTEA extended length of copyright an extra twenty years, one compromise included in the law was to allow libraries to copy, distribute, display, and perform some books within the last twenty years of their copyright term for

Never-Published, Never-Registered Works

Type of work	Copyright term	In the public domain in the U.S. as of 1 January 2020
Unpublished works	Life of the author + 70 years	Works from authors who died before 1950
Unpublished anonymous and pseudonymous works, and works made for hire (corporate authorship)	120 years from date of creation	Works created before 1900
Unpublished works when the death date of the author is not known	120 years from date of creation	Works created before 1900

Works Registered or First Published in the U.S.

Date of publication	Conditions	Copyright term
Before 1925*	None	None. In the public domain due to copyright expiration
1925*–1977	Published without a copyright notice	None. In the public domain due to failure to comply with required formalities
1978–March 1, 1989	Published without notice, and without subsequent registration within 5 years	None. In the public domain due to failure to comply with required formalities
1978–March 1, 1989	Published without notice, but with subsequent registration within 5 years	70 years after the death of author. If a work of corporate authorship: 95 years from publication or 120 years from creation, whichever expires first
1925*–1963	Published with notice but copyright not renewed	None. In the public domain due to copyright expiration

(continued on following page)

TABLE 3.1 Copyright Terms and the Public Domain in the United States

Source: Excerpt of *Copyright Term and the Public Domain in the United States* (citations omitted), © 2002–2021 Peter B. Hirtle, CC BY 3.0 Attribution License, available at https://copyright.cornell.edu/publicdomain.

Works Registered or First Published in the U.S. *(cont.)*

Date of publication	Conditions	Copyright term
1925*–1963	Published with notice and the copyright renewed	95 years after publication date
1964–1977	Published with notice	95 years after publication date
1978–March 1, 1989	Created after 1977 and published with notice	70 years after the death of author. If a work of corporate authorship: 95 years from publication or 120 years from creation, whichever expires first
1978–March 1, 1989	Created before 1978 and first published with notice in the specified period	Either the greater of the term specified in the previous entry or December 31, 2047
March 1, 1989–2002	Created after 1977	70 years after the death of author. If a work of corporate authorship: 95 years from publication or 120 years from creation, whichever expires first
March 1, 1989–2002	Created before 1978 and first published in this period	Either the greater of the term specified in the previous entry or December 31, 2047
After 2002	None	70 years after the death of author. If a work of corporate authorship: 95 years from publication or 120 years from creation, whichever expires first
Anytime	Works prepared by an officer or employee of the United States government as part of that person's official duties	None. In the public domain in the United States (17 U.S.C. § 105)

*Note that the year 1925 is the appropriate year for 2020. In 2021, this date changes to 1926; in 2022 the date changes to 1927, and so on.

"preservation, scholarship, or research."[16] To satisfy Section 108(h), a library or archive may use a published work within the last twenty years of its copyright term when that library or archive has determined, "on the basis of a reasonable investigation," that the work is not "subject to normal commercial exploitation; and a copy . . . of the work can[not] be obtained at a reasonable price."[17] Alternatively, the work cannot be used if the copyright owner of the work has told the Copyright Office that the work is subject to normal commercial exploitation or is available at a reasonable price; however, to date, no such statement has ever been filed with the Copyright Office.[18]

This section requires libraries and archives to check the used market, too, as it does not require the copy of the work obtained at a reasonable price to be a new copy of the work. Note also that this exception does not extend to any subsequent uses beyond the use of the library or archive. However, other users could still rely on fair use.

Pre-1972 Sound Recordings under the Music Modernization Act

The primary purpose of the Music Modernization Act (MMA) was to federalize copyright protection for pre-1972 sound recordings, which were previously protected only under state copyright law. The MMA, however, also has positive implications for libraries and archives. Under Section II of the MMA, the Classics Act, a library or archive can use any published pre-1972 sound recording so long as the institution has determined "on the basis of a reasonable investigation" that the work is not "subject to normal commercial exploitation; and a copy . . . of the work can[not] be obtained at a reasonable price."[19] In other words, the same exception from Section 108(h) applies to all published pre-1972 sound recordings, but the works need not be in their last twenty years of copyright protection for it to apply. Instead, this applies to libraries wishing to copy, distribute, display, and perform any pre-1972 sound recording for "preservation, scholarship, or research."[20]

COMMON SCENARIOS

⊃ **A fellow librarian contacts you to ask whether they can digitize a book published in the United States in 1943 and make the digital copy available to patrons through the library website. Can they?**
The first line of inquiry for works created between 1924 and 1968 is whether the work was a published work. In this case, the inquiry is easy because the book had

a publisher and was widely distributed. The next inquiry is whether the work contained an appropriate copyright notice. You ask the librarian to bring you the book and you are able to determine that nowhere in the book—and especially not on the title page or the page immediately following the title page—is there a copyright notice. Therefore, you determine that the work is in the public domain and the work may be digitized and made available on the library website to the general public, with a note in the metadata that it is in the public domain in the United States.

⊃ **A patron contacts your repository asking you to digitize and make publicly available a dissertation written in 1928, as the current version is available only in print. Can you?**

The first line of inquiry for works created between 1924 and 1968 is whether the work was a published work. For dissertations and theses, it is usually quite difficult to determine just how widely a particular work was distributed in that era. It may also be impossible to find the agreement or license that was signed by the student (if any) when submitting a dissertation or theses at that time. There is a scholarly work on this very issue wherein the authors conclude that dissertations and theses in this era were likely considered "published."[21] If they were considered published and lacked a copyright notice and/or the copyright was not renewed, then the work would be in the public domain and could be digitized. However, this decision will likely be based on each institution. The institution may wish not to digitize all dissertations and theses due to a public relations concern, or may wish to reach out to alumni to alert them to the digitization policy first.

⊃ **A faculty member contacts you to determine if a photograph included in a business pamphlet from 1934 is in the public domain. Where do you begin?**

As you probably know after having read this chapter, this will not be a simple question to solve. But the first question to ask is whether the work was widely distributed or published. Why? Because if it was published, then the work would need to include the required notice of copyright or it would fall into the public domain. However, the notice requirements do not apply to unpublished works. The faculty member confirms that the work was widely distributed, so you examine the work to determine whether notice was properly included. You see on the second page of the work (the page immediately following the title page) a copyright notice © 1934 with the name of the business, so you conclude that notice was properly affixed to the work.

You also know that the photographs included in the work may be owned by another party and could have a different copyright status than the work as a whole. This is the issue known as the "insert" problem. However, in this particular pamphlet, the captions indicate that the photographs were taken at the request of the company: "Photograph produced for (the name of the business) by (the name of the photographer)." You conclude, therefore, that all pamphlet photographs likely constitute a work made for hire. This clears up the issue of having to track down a potential additional copyright notice (under the author's name) for the photograph. If the photograph were not a work made for hire, it could potentially have a different copyright expiration date from the date of the pamphlet. Note that the work in this era (if published) would have the same copyright term whether it was created by an individual author or as a work made for hire.

The next step is to determine whether the registration for the work was properly renewed with the Copyright Office. If so, it would receive the full ninety-five years from the date of publication copyright term. If not, it would be in the public domain.

As the United States Copyright Office notes, "Works published with notice prior to 1978 may be registered at any time within the first 28-year term."[22] Thus, finding the initial copyright registration may be a bit difficult. However, in order to benefit from the extension of copyright to the full ninety-five-year term, the work must have been renewed in the twenty-eighth year of the first term. Thus, searching for the renewal (or lack thereof) would be the easier way to search in this instance.

For a work published in 1934, then, the work should have been renewed by 1962. Searching in the year prior, or 1961, as well as the year following or 1963 is recommended to be thorough. So, for this particular work, you would look for renewal records for "pamphlets" in 1961 through 1963 under the business name and/or the title of the pamphlet.

But where can you search? Currently, the United States Copyright Office does not include a searchable database for copyright records before 1978. Therefore, the best place to search is the online Catalogue of Copyright Entries (CCE), which is available in a searchable format through the University of Pennsylvania at https://onlinebooks.library.upenn.edu/cce/.

Note that to effectively search the CCE, you must know the year you are searching, as well as the type of work and the author or title of the work.

After having searched under renewal records for pamphlets in 1961, 1962, and 1963 using the name of the business as well as the title of the book and the title of the photograph, and finding no results, you are satisfied that this work is indeed in the public domain—although sometimes works may be misfiled in the CCE records, and it may be worthwhile to search in the copyright renewal records for books, too. The United States Copyright Office cautions that these searches are imperfect by nature, and it is much harder to prove a negative than a positive, so it is best to be cautiously optimistic with a negative search result.

One final note about searching for copyright renewal records: Stanford University has a wonderful copyright renewal search database that is much easier to use than the CCE, at https://library.stanford.edu/collections/copyright -renewal-database. However, it is valid only for type A works—namely, books published in the United States between the years 1923 and 1963.

TOOLS & RESOURCES

Bartlett, Bernadette, Kyle Courtney, Kristina Eden, and Kris Kasianovitz. Free State Government Information. http://stategov.freegovinfo.info.

This website provides additional information about the public domain status of state government documents.

Brewer, Michael, and the ALA Office for Information Technology Policy. Digital Copyright Slider Tool. 2020. Available at https://100pianos.com/drafts/ digitalslider/index.html. CC-BY-NC-SA.

This slider tool is helpful for determining when a United States work is in the public domain.

CENDI. *Frequently Asked Questions about Copyright: Issues Affecting the U.S. Government.* 2017. https://cendi.gov/publications/FAQ_Copyright_30jan18.pdf.

This document provides common questions and answers about U.S. governmental copyright issues.

Hirtle, Peter. *Copyright Term and the Public Domain in the United States.* https://copyright.cornell.edu/publicdomain.

The public domain chart (shown in table 3.1) is extremely useful in determining whether a work is in the public domain.

Office for Scholarly Communication, Harvard Library. State Copyright Resource Center. http://copyright.lib.harvard.edu/states/.

Kyle Courtney and Katie Zimmerman have created an interactive map linking to relevant case law and legislative documents detailing the public domain status of state government documents.

Townsend Gard, Elizabeth. "Creating a Last (L20) Collection: Implementing Section 108(h) in Libraries, Archives, and Museums." Paper, October 2, 2017. http://dx.doi.org/10.2139/ssrn.3049158.

This paper provides more information about works in the pseudo public domain for libraries under Section 108(h) of the Copyright Act.

Samuelson Law, Technology & Public Policy Clinic. *Is It in the Public Domain? A Handbook for Evaluating the Copyright Status of a Work Created in the United States between January 1, 1923 and December 31, 1977.* Berkeley Law, University of California, 2014. https://www.law.berkeley.edu/files/ FINAL_PublicDomain_Handbook_FINAL(1).pdf.

This handbook helps librarians determine whether a work created in the United States between 1925 and 1977 is in the public domain.

U.S. Copyright Office. *Compendium of U.S. Copyright Office Practices*, 3rd ed. Washington, D.C.: U.S. Copyright Office, 2021. https://www.copyright.gov/comp3/.

The *Compendium* contains helpful information about publication status in chapter 1900 (for works first published on or after January 1, 1978), chapter 2100 (for earlier works), and chapter 1000 (for online works).

U.S. Copyright Office. *Duration of Copyright.* Circulation 15A, reviewed 2011. https://www.copyright.gov/circs/circ15a.pdf.

This circular provides information on the duration (or length) of copyright.

U.S. Copyright Office. *Extension of Copyright Terms.* Circular 15T, revised 2010. https://www.copyright.gov/circs/circ15t.pdf.

This circular provides information on the extension of copyright terms for works copyrighted before 1978.

U.S. Copyright Office. "Notice of Inquiry for Online Publication." *Federal Register* 84, no. 23 (December 3, 2019). https://www.govinfo.gov/content/ pkg/FR-2019-12-04/pdf/2019-26004.pdf.

When the Copyright Office conducted a study about what constitutes online publication, the call for public comment provided a thorough summary of the law relating to publication in the digital environment.

U.S. Copyright Office. *Renewal Registration.* Circular 6A, revised 2021. https://www.copyright.gov/circs/circ06a.pdf.

This circular provides information on the effect of copyright renewal of copyright for works copyrighted between 1964 and 1977.

NOTES

1. United States Copyright Office, "Definitions," https://www.copyright.gov/help/faq/faq-definitions.html.

2. Edward Lee, "The Public Domain: The Evolution of Legal Restraints on the Government's Power to Control Public Access through Secrecy or Intellectual Property," *Hastings Law Journal* 55 (2003): 91–209.

3. 17 U.S.C. § 105(b)–(c).

4. *Georgia v. Public.Resource.Org, Inc.*, 140 S.Ct. 1498 (2020).

5. *Id.*

6. 17 U.S.C. § 305.

7. 17 U.S.C. § 402(c).

8. 17 U.S.C. § 405(a)(2).

9. 17 U.S.C. § 101.

10. *Id.*

11. Deborah R. Gerhardt, "Copyright Publication: An Empirical Study," *Notre Dame Law Review* 87, no. 1 (2013): 149.

12. *King v. Mister Maestro, Inc.*, 224 F. Supp. 101 (S.D.N.Y. 1963).

13. *White v. Kimmel*, 193 F.2d 744 (9th Cir. 1952).

14. United States Copyright Office, "Notice of Inquiry for Online Publication," *Federal Register* 84, no. 23 (December 3, 2019), https://www.govinfo.gov/content/pkg/FR-2019-12-04/pdf/2019-26004.pdf.

15. See U.S. Copyright Office, *Compendium of U.S. Copyright Office Practices*, 3rd. ed. (2021), § 1902.

16. 17 U.S.C. § 108(h).

17. *Id.*

18. U.S. Copyright Office, *Section 108 of Title 17: A Discussion Document of the Register of Copyrights* (2017), https://www.copyright.gov/policy/section108/discussion-document.pdf.

19. *Id.*

20. 17 U.S.C. § 108(h).

21. Gail Clement and Melissa Levine, "Copyright and Publication Status of Pre-1978 Dissertations: A Content Analysis Approach," *portal: Libraries and the Academy* 11, no. 3 (2011): 825.

22. U.S. Copyright Office. *How to Investigate the Copyright Status of a Work*. Circular 22, revised 2013. https://www.copyright.gov/circs/circ22.pdf, 3.

CHAPTER 4

Making Copies for Preservation

Title 17, Section 108: Limitations on Exclusive Rights—Reproductions by Libraries and Archives

(a) Except as otherwise provided in this title and notwithstanding the provisions of section 106, it is not an infringement of copyright for a library or archives, or any of its employees acting within the scope of their employment, to reproduce no more than one copy or phonorecord of a work, except as provided in subsections (b) and (c), or to distribute such copy or phonorecord, under the conditions specified by this section, if—

   (1) the reproduction or distribution is made without any purpose of direct or indirect commercial advantage;

   (2) the collections of the library or archives are

       (i) open to the public, or

       (ii) available not only to researchers affiliated with the library or archives or with the institution of which it is a part, but also to other persons doing research in a specialized field; and

   (3) the reproduction or distribution of the work includes a notice of copyright that appears on the copy or phonorecord that is reproduced under the provisions of this section, or includes a legend stating that the work may be protected by copyright if no such notice can be found on the copy or phonorecord that is reproduced under the provisions of this section.

(b) The rights of reproduction and distribution under this section apply to three copies or phonorecords of an unpublished work duplicated solely for purposes of preservation and security or for deposit for research use in another library or archives of the type described by clause (2) of subsection (a), if—

   (1) the copy or phonorecord reproduced is currently in the collections of the library or archives; and

(2) any such copy or phonorecord that is reproduced in digital format is not otherwise distributed in that format and is not made available to the public in that format outside the premises of the library or archives.

(c) The right of reproduction under this section applies to three copies or phonorecords of a published work duplicated solely for the purpose of replacement of a copy or phonorecord that is damaged, deteriorating, lost, or stolen, or if the existing format in which the work is stored has become obsolete, if—

(1) the library or archives has, after a reasonable effort, determined that an unused replacement cannot be obtained at a fair price; and

(2) any such copy or phonorecord that is reproduced in digital format is not made available to the public in that format outside the premises of the library or archives in lawful possession of such copy.

For purposes of this subsection, a format shall be considered obsolete if the machine or device necessary to render perceptible a work stored in that format is no longer manufactured or is no longer reasonably available in the commercial marketplace.

. . .

(f) Nothing in this section—

(1) shall be construed to impose liability for copyright infringement upon a library or archives or its employees for the unsupervised use of reproducing equipment located on its premises: *Provided*, That such equipment displays a notice that the making of a copy may be subject to the copyright law;

(2) excuses a person who uses such reproducing equipment or who requests a copy or phonorecord under subsection (d) from liability for copyright infringement for any such act, or for any later use of such copy or phonorecord, if it exceeds fair use as provided by section 107;

(3) shall be construed to limit the reproduction and distribution by lending of a limited number of copies and excerpts by a library or archives of an audiovisual news program, subject to clauses (1), (2), and (3) of subsection (a); or

(4) in any way affects the right of fair use as provided by section 107, or any contractual obligations assumed at any time by the library or archives when it obtained a copy or phonorecord of a work in its collections.

DISCUSSION OF THE LAW

There is a lot of information packed into Section 108 of the Copyright Act, and all of it pertains to libraries and archives, so it is important to understand this portion. It begins in Subsection (a) by defining the types of institutions that qualify for the ability to make certain copies (for preservation) without penalty as an exception to the Copyright Act. One thing you will note immediately is that nowhere in this section does the act mention museums; it is limited on its face to libraries and archives.

This exception to the Copyright Act, which allows for certain preservation copies to be made by libraries and archives, is limited to those institutions that are open to the public or that allow other researchers doing work in a specialized field to enter the premises to do research. Additionally, the copies protected under this section must be made for a research purpose with no commercial purpose and all copies must have a proper copyright notice attached to them.

Preservation of Unpublished Works

The rules for making copies for preservation of unpublished works are a bit less strenuous and easier to satisfy in any given instance than the rules for preservation of published works. Why? A given copy of an unpublished work may be the only copy of that particular work in the world, and we want to encourage the preservation of that work through archival copies.

Thus, a librarian or archivist need only demonstrate, under Title 17 of the U.S. Code, Section 108(b), that they are making a copy of an unpublished work for preservation to make up to three copies of the work. Similarly, the limited copies may be made to share with another library for deposit for research purposes as well. The unpublished work (and the copy made of the work) must currently be in the collections of the library or archives and any digital copies made of the work may only be shared on the premises of the library or archives.

Please note that scholars have acknowledged that in the digital age it is almost impossible to limit a "digital copy" such as a PDF to three copies, as there will be backup copies imprinted on servers. Scholars have also acknowledged that the "premises" of the library or archives is not defined in the act and, as such, has been interpreted in a variety of ways, including the physical premises (with an individual computer dedicated to viewing unpublished digital copies of works in the library or archives) as well as the digital premises (including anywhere that an authorized patron can log in to the library or archival collection).[1]

Preservation of Published Works

Section 108(c) addresses the preservation of published works and is a bit more involved because it is not meant to allow for general copying of published works that would interfere with the commercial value of the works. Thus up to three copies of a published work may be made for preservation purposes if the copy of the work is lost, deteriorating, or stolen and "the library or archives has, after a reasonable effort, determined that an unused replacement cannot be obtained at a fair price" and the digital copy, if any, of the work is not made available outside of the premises of the library or archives. Note that the library or archives must make a reasonable effort to search for a fairly priced new version of the published work and need not search the used marketplace. The librarian or archivist should use good judgment when determining whether a particular price is a fair price for a new copy of the work.

COMMON SCENARIOS

⊃ **An archival department of the library has the only copy of a letter written by a famous author in its collection and is concerned about the letter deteriorating. The archives does not own the copyright for the work, and it is still in copyright. Can the archives make a copy of the letter? If so, in what format? What can the archives do with that copy of the letter?**

With unpublished and unique works, the exception to copyright for preservation is strong because the work may otherwise deteriorate and be lost. Thus, the answer is a definite yes to making a copy of the work for preservation purposes without being concerned about violating copyright. In fact, Section 108 provides that the archive may make up to three copies of the work for preservation purposes. However, in modern times, with scanning and backup copies on computer drives, we know that this requirement of up to three copies is rather restrictive. In practice, many archives do not restrict themselves to the three-copy limit because where the protections of Section 108 end, fair use begins. To that end, making copies for preservation to preserve the historical record for scholars and researchers is generally considered a fair use by the academic community. Thus the copies could be photocopies, but need not necessarily be limited to that format, and many modern archives make the copies in electronic form. Of course, patrons may access the electronic copy of the letter, but only on the premises of the library. How broadly a given institution interprets the phrase "the premises of the library" varies, from limiting patron access to computers within the physical location of the library to logging on to a virtual library space on the internet.

⊃ **A librarian from a middle school library wishes to make copies of DVDs because students often lose the copies that are checked out. Can they make such copies to have a backup in case one is lost?**

No. Although the preservation provisions of Section 108 do allow libraries to make copies of books that were lost or stolen if they cannot purchase another copy at a reasonable price, those provisions do not apply to audiovisual works, pursuant to Section 108(i). Additionally, copies cannot be made in advance of a work being lost or stolen.

⊃ **A librarian receives a notification that a relatively rare (no longer sold commercially) book has been lost by a patron. He is able to borrow a copy of the book from another library. Can the librarian make a copy of the entire book to replace the lost book?**

Likely, he may do so. The librarian, of course, can borrow a book if the lending library is willing to ship the physical book to them using the Right of First Sale. If not, he might be able to request the entire copy of the book through interlibrary loan. However, the book could only be copied if under Section 108(e) the librarian cannot find a copy (used or new) of the work available at a fair price. That same requirement applies to the preservation copy under Section 108(c); however, the librarian must look for a new or unused copy of the book in the commercial marketplace. In this case, assuming that the book is no longer being printed, it is unlikely a new copy of the book could be obtained at a fair price. Note, however, the restriction on how the replacement copy can be circulated. Any digital copy of the book may not be viewable outside the premises of the library. As noted in the discussion above, interpretations of this clause vary, from looking at the work on a computer in the physical library to looking at a "view-only" copy of the digital book through an internet portal to the library.

TOOLS & RESOURCES

University of Illinois at Urbana–Champaign Library. *Copyright and Digitization of Library Materials Library Guide.* https://guides.library.illinois.edu/digitizationoflibrarymaterials/section108.

This is a helpful library guide about Section 108 of the Copyright Act created for librarians wishing to digitize library collections.

U.S. Copyright Office. *Section 108 of Title 17. A Discussion Document of the Register of Copyrights* (2017). https://www.copyright.gov/policy/section108/discussion-document.pdf.

This resource serves as a very good summary of Section 108 of the Copyright Act. Note that in addition to discussing the law as it currently stands, the *Discussion Document* includes suggestions for possible changes to Section 108 (possible amendments to the law) and as such, the document should be read carefully so as not to confuse the discussion of possible amendments with the law as it now stands.

NOTE

1. U.S. Copyright Office, *Section 108 of Title 17: A Discussion Document of the Register of Copyrights* (2017), 18n82, https://www.copyright.gov/policy/section108/discussion-document.pdf.

CHAPTER 5

Interlibrary Loan and Unsupervised Patron Copying

THE LAW

Title 17, Section 108: Limitations on Exclusive Rights—Reproductions by Libraries and Archives

(a) Except as otherwise provided in this title and notwithstanding the provisions of section 106, it is not an infringement of copyright for a library or archives, or any of its employees acting within the scope of their employment, to reproduce no more than one copy or phonorecord of a work, except as provided in subsections (b) and (c), or to distribute such copy or phonorecord, under the conditions specified by this section, if—

   (1) the reproduction or distribution is made without any purpose of direct or indirect commercial advantage;

   (2) the collections of the library or archives are

      (i) open to the public, or

      (ii) available not only to researchers affiliated with the library or archives or with the institution of which it is a part, but also to other persons doing research in a specialized field; and

   (3) the reproduction or distribution of the work includes a notice of copyright that appears on the copy or phonorecord that is reproduced under the provisions of this section, or includes a legend stating that the work may be protected by copyright if no such notice can be found on the copy or phonorecord that is reproduced under the provisions of this section.

. . .

(d) The rights of reproduction and distribution under this section apply to a copy, made from the collection of a library or archives where the user makes his or her request or from that of another library or archives, of no more than one article or other contribution to a copyrighted collection or periodical issue, or to a copy or phonorecord of a small part of any other copyrighted work, if—

(1) the copy or phonorecord becomes the property of the user, and the library or archives has had no notice that the copy or phonorecord would be used for any purpose other than private study, scholarship, or research; and

(2) the library or archives displays prominently, at the place where orders are accepted, and includes on its order form, a warning of copyright in accordance with requirements that the Register of Copyrights shall prescribe by regulation.

(e) The rights of reproduction and distribution under this section apply to the entire work, or to a substantial part of it, made from the collection of a library or archives where the user makes his or her request or from that of another library or archives, if the library or archives has first determined, on the basis of a reasonable investigation, that a copy or phonorecord of the copyrighted work cannot be obtained at a fair price, if—

(1) the copy or phonorecord becomes the property of the user, and the library or archives has had no notice that the copy or phonorecord would be used for any purpose other than private study, scholarship, or research; and

(2) the library or archives displays prominently, at the place where orders are accepted, and includes on its order form, a warning of copyright in accordance with requirements that the Register of Copyrights shall prescribe by regulation.

(f) Nothing in this section—

(1) shall be construed to impose liability for copyright infringement upon a library or archives or its employees for the unsupervised use of reproducing equipment located on its premises: *Provided*, That such equipment displays a notice that the making of a copy may be subject to the copyright law;

(2) excuses a person who uses such reproducing equipment or who requests a copy or phonorecord under subsection (d) from liability for copyright infringement for any such act, or for any later use of such copy or phonorecord, if it exceeds fair use as provided by section 107;

(3) shall be construed to limit the reproduction and distribution by lending of a limited number of copies and excerpts by a library or archives of an audiovisual news program, subject to clauses (1), (2), and (3) of subsection (a); or

(4) in any way affects the right of fair use as provided by section 107, or any contractual obligations assumed at any time by the library or archives when it obtained a copy or phonorecord of a work in its collections.

(g) The rights of reproduction and distribution under this section extend to the isolated and unrelated reproduction or distribution of a single copy or phonorecord of the same material on separate occasions, but do not extend to cases where the library or archives, or its employee—

(1) is aware or has substantial reason to believe that it is engaging in the related or concerted reproduction or distribution of multiple copies or phonorecords of the same material, whether made on one occasion or over a period of time, and whether intended for aggregate use by one or more individuals or for separate use by the individual members of a group; or

(2) engages in the systematic reproduction or distribution of single or multiple copies or phonorecords of material described in subsection (d): *Provided*, That nothing in this clause prevents a library or archives from participating in interlibrary arrangements that do not have, as their purpose or effect, that the library or archives receiving such copies or phonorecords for distribution does so in such aggregate quantities as to substitute for a subscription to or purchase of such work.

...

(i) The rights of reproduction and distribution under this section do not apply to a musical work, a pictorial, graphic or sculptural work, or a motion picture or other audiovisual work other than an audiovisual work dealing with news, except that no such limitation shall apply with respect to rights granted by subsections (b), (c), and (h), or with respect to pictorial or graphic works published as illustrations, diagrams, or similar adjuncts to works of which copies are reproduced or distributed in accordance with subsections (d) and (e).

DISCUSSION OF THE LAW

Patron Copying

Libraries often have copy machines available for patron use. Well-meaning librarians are often tempted to advise patrons on their overuse of the machines and the line between appropriate (fair use) and copyright infringement. However, Section 108 of the Copyright Act provides that libraries are not liable for the "unsupervised use" of copy equipment in the library. In other words, if you have a copyright notice posted near a copy machine, book scanner, or other copy equipment in your library space and a patron copies too much of a book, video, or other copyrighted work, the library is not legally responsible for that copyright violation. Note that this requires two things: (1) a copyright notice to be placed near the copy equipment; and (2) the use of copy equipment that is unsupervised by library employees. Although it can be tempting to tell a patron to stop copying an entire book, the library is in a better legal position if library employees do not supervise the equipment and do allow patrons to make their own fair use and copyright assessments. Figure 5.1 shows one approach for delivering this message.

Interlibrary Loan

The interlibrary loan section of the act can be thought of as broken into two distinct sections with an overarching set of principles that apply to the entire section. This discussion, then, will begin with the overarching principles and

THE LAW REQUIRES THAT WE TELL YOU THIS:

Copyright Notice for Unsupervised Copying Equipment:

The copyright law of the United States (Title 17, U.S. Code) governs the making of photocopies or other reproductions of copyrighted material; the person using this equipment is liable for any infringement.

THE LAW DOES NOT REQUIRE THAT WE TELL YOU THIS:

The law is not only for copyright holders. Users have rights too.

Fair use (Title 17, U.S. Code §107) allows users to make certain uses of copyrighted works without permission. **Learn about fair use and then use your best judgment.**

Learn more: www.go.osu.edu/copyright

KNOW YOUR COPYRIGHTS

FIGURE 5.1 Example of sign for unsupervised copy machine

Source: Ohio State University Library, unsupervised copy machine sign, modified from University of Michigan Copyright Office under a CC BY license.

then continue with the more specific sections applying to copies of limited portions of a work versus entire works.

One of the limiting factors for interlibrary loan (ILL) is provided in Subsection (i) of Section 108. That subsection states that the copyright exception allowing librarians to make and distribute copies to another patron or library for the purpose of research or scholarship does not apply to musical works, pictorial, graphic or sculptural works, or audiovisual works or movies. The term "musical works" is not defined in the Copyright Act itself, but the Copyright Office defines it in the *Compendium* as "songs, song lyrics, symphonies, concertos, advertising jingles, and similar types of musical works."[1] This, of course, is distinguishable from "sound recordings," which are defined in the Copyright Act and do qualify for ILL. Due to this exclusion, libraries typically will exercise the right of first sale to lend published, purchased sheet music between one library and another (with the expectation that the lent music will be returned to the lending library) or make a copy of the sheet music under a fair use analysis. Similarly, one library cannot make a copy of a copyright-protected movie for the purpose of lending it to a patron through another library (at least, not without some other justification, such as Section 108[h] permitting works within the last twenty years of copyright protection to be copied when other conditions are met). Note that audiovisual news is excluded from the limitation in subsection (i) and may be lent or copied for the purpose of library lending.

Another overarching principle regarding ILL is that libraries are not allowed to use it to "substitute for a subscription to or purchase of" the works they are requesting through ILL from other libraries. While a library may request the same item through ILL on multiple occasions due to genuine patron requests, these requests should be "isolated and unrelated" and not "concerted reproduction or distribution of the same material." These rules have led to the development of guidelines by the Commission on New Technology Uses of Copyrighted Works in 1978 (CONTU Guidelines). The CONTU Guidelines have mistakenly been cited as law by many; but in fact, they are simply guidelines intended to satisfy the law. Thus, things such as the "rule of five"—whereby the requesting library may not receive more than five copies of any one periodical title whose publication date falls within the previous five years of the date of the patron's ILL request—have been ingrained into the practices of ILL librarians and have caused them to unnecessarily pay additional licensing fees when using ILL.

Complicating the fact that the CONTU Guidelines were never law, they are now outdated as well. It is no longer valid to assume that the licensing cost of five articles per year would exceed the cost of a journal subscription, due to the increasing cost of journal licensing (which is the rationale for the CONTU Guideline's rule of five mentioned above). Instead of complying with the CONTU Guidelines, however, libraries should follow copyright law—including fair use—in exercising ILL practices. Of course, a risk-averse library may still wish to continue relying on the CONTU Guidelines if it does not feel comfortable taking a more nuanced approach to analyzing ILL usage.

COMMON SCENARIOS

⊃ A patron requests a digitized copy of an unpublished musical score through ILL. Can the library make a copy or send the original score to the patron through ILL?

Under Section 108 of the Copyright Act, musical works, such as sheet music or scores, are not part of the library ILL exception to copyright. Therefore, generally, in order to lend a musical score between libraries, the lending library would rely on the first sale doctrine, or Section 109 of the Copyright Act, by lending the original score (and not a copy). However, if the musical score is unpublished, it is more likely to be too unique and valuable for the lending library to circulate. In that instance, if the requesting patron or library can secure permission from the copyright owner, then a copy could be made to provide to the patron so that the lending library is able to retain the original unpublished work.[2]

⊃ A professor requests a copy of an article from a scholarly journal that her library does not subscribe to through ILL. Can the professor use that copy for electronic reserves for her class?

Under the ILL provisions of the Copyright Act, the professor may request an article from a scholarly journal for private study, scholarship, or research. If the professor has requested an article properly through ILL, the professor could then make a determination as to whether the use would be justified for educational use as a fair use. If the professor makes the good-faith determination that the use would be a fair use, then the professor could use that copy for the classroom. For further information about how to properly assess fair use, see chapter 8, "The TEACH Act."

⊃ A librarian is working at an information desk near a book-scanning machine in the library. The librarian sees a patron scanning large

portions of a book. Should they intervene and explain to the patron that this may violate copyright law?

No. As long as the scanner has an appropriate copyright notice, the librarian should not supervise copying made on the machine. The role of the librarian may be to answer questions about how to use the machine or even to provide informational resources about fair use or copyright permissions to the patron when approached by the patron; but the librarian is actually creating potential liability for the library if they supervise copying on the machine. Indeed, the Copyright Act provides for a limitation of library liability for unsupervised copy equipment when the appropriate copyright notice is properly located near the machine. Therefore, the librarian should not intervene here.

TOOLS & RESOURCES

Crews, Kenneth D., and Dwayne K. Buttler. Copyright Checklist for Libraries: Providing Copies for Private Study. Copyright Advisory Office, Columbia University Libraries, last revised 2009. CC BY 4.0. https://library.columbia.edu/content/dam/libraryweb/services/preservation/copyrightchecklist108privatestudy.pdf.

Kenneth Crews and Dwayne Buttler, copyright experts, developed a helpful checklist for libraries providing copies of works in their collection to patrons for private study pursuant Sections 108(d) and 108(e) of the Copyright Act. The checklist is reprinted for ease of access (and copying) in appendix A of this book.

Myers, Carla. *Copyright and Course Reserves: Legal Issues and Best Practices for Academic Libraries.* Santa Barbara: ABC-CLIO, 2021.

This book includes a deep dive into the world of copyright and course reserves.

Oakley, Meg, Laura Quilter, and Sara Benson. "Modern Interlibrary Loan Practices: Moving beyond the CONTU Guidelines." White paper, Association of Research Libraries, Washington, D.C., August 31, 2020. https://doi.org/10.29242/report.contu2020.

This white paper summarizes why the CONTU Guidelines are outdated and provides libraries with an alternate way to analyze interlibrary loan under Section 108 and fair use.

NOTES

1. U.S. Copyright Office, *Compendium of U.S. Copyright Office Practices*, 3rd ed. (2021), § 503.1(B).
2. I want to thank Nazareth Pantaloni III, associate librarian at the Indiana University Bloomington, as well as Kenneth Crews, an attorney with Gipson Hoffman & Pancione, for their input on this hypothetical situation.

CHAPTER 6

Access to Copyrighted Material for Patrons with Disabilities

Title 17, Section 121: Limitations on Exclusive Rights—Reproduction for Blind or Other People with Disabilities

(a) Notwithstanding the provisions of section 106, it is not an infringement of copyright for an authorized entity to reproduce or to distribute in the United States copies or phonorecords of a previously published literary work or of a previously published musical work that has been fixed in the form of text or notation if such copies or phonorecords are reproduced or distributed in accessible formats exclusively for use by eligible persons.

(b)

   (1) Copies or phonorecords to which this section applies shall—

      (A) not be reproduced or distributed in the United States in a format other than an accessible format exclusively for use by eligible persons;

      (B) bear a notice that any further reproduction or distribution in a format other than an accessible format is an infringement; and

      (C) include a copyright notice identifying the copyright owner and the date of the original publication.

   (2) The provisions of this subsection shall not apply to standardized, secure, or norm-referenced tests and related testing material, or to computer programs, except the portions thereof that are in conventional human language (including descriptions of pictorial works) and displayed to users in the ordinary course of using the computer programs.

(c) Notwithstanding the provisions of section 106, it is not an infringement of copyright for a publisher of print instructional materials for use in elementary or secondary schools to create and distribute to the National Instructional Materials Access Center copies of the electronic files described in sections 612(a)(23)(C), 613(a)(6), and section 674(e) of the Individuals with

Disabilities Education Act that contain the contents of print instructional materials using the National Instructional Material Accessibility Standard (as defined in section 674(e)(3) of that Act), if—

(1) the inclusion of the contents of such print instructional materials is required by any State educational agency or local educational agency;

(2) the publisher had the right to publish such print instructional materials in print formats; and

(3) such copies are used solely for reproduction or distribution of the contents of such print instructional materials in accessible formats.

(d) For purposes of this section, the term—

(1) "accessible format" means an alternative manner or form that gives an eligible person access to the work when the copy or phonorecord in the accessible format is used exclusively by the eligible person to permit him or her to have access as feasibly and comfortably as a person without such disability as described in paragraph (3);

(2) "authorized entity" means a nonprofit organization or a governmental agency that has a primary mission to provide specialized services relating to training, education, or adaptive reading or information access needs of blind or other persons with disabilities;

(3) "eligible person" means an individual who, regardless of any other disability—

(A) is blind;

(B) has a visual impairment or perceptual or reading disability that cannot be improved to give visual function substantially equivalent to that of a person who has no such impairment or disability and so is unable to read printed works to substantially the same degree as a person without an impairment or disability; or

(C) is otherwise unable, through physical disability, to hold or manipulate a book or to focus or move the eyes to the extent that would be normally acceptable for reading; and

(4) "print instructional materials" has the meaning given under section 674(e)(3)(C) of the Individuals with Disabilities Education Act.

Title 20, Section 1474(e)(3)(c): Print Instructional Materials

The term "print instructional materials" means printed textbooks and related printed core materials that are written and published primarily for use in elementary school and secondary school instruction and are required by a State educational agency or local educational agency for use by students in the classroom.

Title 17, Section 121A: Limitation on Exclusive Rights—Reproduction for Blind or Other People with Disabilities in Marrakesh Treaty Countries

(a) Notwithstanding the provisions of sections 106 and 602 [the exclusive rights under copyright and the sections discussing infringing importation/exportation of copyrighted materials], it is not an infringement of copyright for an authorized entity, acting pursuant to this section, to export copies or phonorecords of a previously published literary work or of a previously published musical work that has been fixed in the form of text or notation in accessible formats to another country when the exportation is made either to—

    (1)   an authorized entity located in a country that is a Party to the Marrakesh Treaty; or

    (2)   an eligible person in a country that is a Party to the Marrakesh Treaty,

        if prior to the exportation of such copies or phonorecords, the authorized entity engaged in the exportation did not know or have reasonable grounds to know that the copies or phonorecords would be used other than by eligible persons.

(b)   Notwithstanding the provisions of sections 106 and 602, it is not an infringement of copyright for an authorized entity or an eligible person, or someone acting on behalf of an eligible person, acting pursuant to this section, to import copies or phonorecords of a previously published literary work or of a previously published musical work that has been fixed in the form of text or notation in accessible formats.

(c)   In conducting activities under subsection (a) or (b), an authorized entity shall establish and follow its own practices, in keeping with its particular circumstances, to—

    (1)   establish that the persons the authorized entity serves are eligible persons;

    (2)   limit to eligible persons and authorized entities the distribution of accessible format copies by the authorized entity;

    (3)   discourage the reproduction and distribution of unauthorized copies;

    (4)   maintain due care in, and records of, the handling of copies of works by the authorized entity, while respecting the privacy of eligible persons on an equal basis with others; and

    (5)   facilitate effective cross-border exchange of accessible format copies by making publicly available—

        (A)   the titles of works for which the authorized entity has accessible format copies or phonorecords and the specific accessible formats in which they are available; and

        (B)   information on the policies, practices, and authorized entity partners of the authorized entity for the cross-border exchange of accessible format copies.

. . .

(e)   Nothing in this section shall be construed to limit the ability to engage in any activity otherwise permitted under this title.

(f)   For purposes of this section—

    (1)   the terms "accessible format", "authorized entity", and "eligible person" have the meanings given those terms in section 121; and

    (2)   the term "Marrakesh Treaty" means the Marrakesh Treaty to Facilitate Access to Published Works by Visually Impaired Persons and Persons with Print Disabilities concluded at Marrakesh, Morocco, on June 28, 2013.

DISCUSSION OF THE LAW

Library patrons may have difficulty reading a print or electronic work available through the library (or listening to a sound recording available through the library) due to a physical disability. Library patrons may have difficulty using library materials for a variety of reasons, including an inability to physically hold a print copy of a book; blind or visually impaired patrons have difficulty accessing more traditional library materials and may need to use a screen reader to listen to the text as it is read aloud. The Copyright Act permits libraries to provide authorized individuals (those with disabilities preventing them from accessing the work) with copies of the work that are compatible with audio readers and the like.

There are, of course, a few requirements to comply with the disability-access provisions of the Copyright Act. Naturally, the library cannot unilaterally copy materials that are in copyright to make them accessible to disabled patrons. These provisions of the Copyright Act are triggered when an eligible person (a person suffering from a disability that interferes with their ability to access the work) contacts the library requesting an accessible copy. Libraries have varying practices regarding whether they require any "proof" of disability; however, the law itself does not require that the lending library maintain any records of such proof, and, as such, many libraries take the patron at their word when they state that they have a disability and necessitate a screen-reader-compatible copy of the work. The lending library must also include a copyright notice on the accessible copy, as well as a notice that reproduction in any other manner besides an accessible format is impermissible.

In addition to the specific exception to copyright law provided in Section 121 of the Copyright Act, it is important to note that making copies available to patrons with visual impairments is also a fair use.[1]

Recently, the United States enacted legislation to codify our accession to the Marrakesh Treaty in Section 121A of the Copyright Act. The legislation had the force of law as of May 8, 2019. Under the treaty, contracting states can transfer accessible works between libraries across international borders. Thus, accessible copies can be provided to library patrons not only in the United States, but internationally to "authorized entities" and individuals in countries that have ratified the treaty as well. The provisions in Section 121A, then, are very similar to those in Section 121 of the Copyright Act, but they authorize the transfer of copies enabling individuals with disabilities between countries that have ratified the treaty to have access copies from other nations.

The statute notes authorized entities should establish a procedure to maintain their own records regarding how they are determining that copies are serving "eligible persons." An "authorized entity," as noted in Subsection (d)(2) of Section 121, is "a nonprofit organization or a governmental agency that has a primary mission to provide specialized services relating to training, education, or adaptive reading or information access needs of blind or other persons with disabilities." The authorized entity should also limit distribution to eligible persons; discourage reproduction/distribution of unauthorized copies; maintain records, while respecting patrons' privacy, of the handling of copies of works for eligible persons; and facilitate international sharing of works in accessible formats by publicly showing lists of titles of accessibly formatted works, as well as "information on the policies, practices, and authorized entity partners of the authorized entity for the cross-border exchange of accessible format copies."

COMMON SCENARIOS

⊃ **A patron contacts the library asking for a screen-reader-compatible version of the third Harry Potter book because she is visually impaired. Can you provide her with a screen-reader-accessible copy?**

As long as the library is a nonprofit organization providing information access to persons with disabilities and the patron making the request is an eligible person under the act, the answer is yes. As noted in the above discussion, the policies of different libraries vary, relating to whether they require any "proof" of disability; but generally it is acceptable to take the patron at their word. Of course, the copy of the work in the accessible format must include a copyright notice as well as a notice that it may not be further reproduced or distributed.

⊃ **A library in Sweden contacts your library asking for a screen-reader-compatible version of the Harry Potter series for a patron who is visually impaired. Can you provide the library with a screen-reader-accessible copy of the series?**

If Sweden has also implemented the Marrakesh Treaty and the request was made by an "authorized entity," the copy of the series may be provided. At the time of writing, Sweden has not signed the treaty, therefore the copy cannot be provided.

⊃ **A patron contacts the library asking for subtitles to be added to a movie that is available for checkout. Can your library add closed captions to the movie?**

No, not under these provisions of the Copyright Act. They apply only to literary works or published musical works. Your library may, however, be able to make a copy of the movie to add closed captions under exceptions to the Digital Millennium Copyright Act (DMCA), as long as the vendor of the movie does not sell a copy of the movie with closed captions at a reasonable price.

TOOLS & RESOURCES

U.S. Copyright Office. "Understanding the Marrakesh Treaty Implementation Act." August 2020. https://www.copyright.gov/legislation/2018_marrakesh _faqs.pdf.

This is a short guide to frequently asked questions and answers about the Marrakesh Treaty Implementation Act.

World Intellectual Property Organization. Marrakesh Treaty to Facilitate Access to Published Works for Persons Who Are Blind, Visually Impaired, or Otherwise Print Disabled. https://www.wipo.int/treaties/en/ip/ marrakesh/.

WIPO provides more information on the Marrakesh Treaty, as well as an updated list of countries that have signed the treaty.

NOTE

1. *Authors Guild, Inc. v. HathiTrust*, 755 F.3d 87, 102 (2d Cir. 2014).

CHAPTER 7

Face-to-Face Teaching versus Public Performance Rights

Title 17, Section 110(1): Limitations on Exclusive Rights—Exemption of Certain Performances or Displays

Notwithstanding the provisions of section 106, the following are not infringements of copyright:

(1) performance or display of a work by instructors or pupils in the course of face-to-face teaching activities of a nonprofit educational institution, in a classroom or similar place devoted to instruction, unless, in the case of a motion picture or other audiovisual work, the performance, or the display of individual images, is given by means of a copy that was not lawfully made under this title, and that the person responsible for the performance knew or had reason to believe was not lawfully made[.]

House of Representatives, 94th Congress 2d Session, House Report No. 94-1476 (1976) (Legislative History of Section 110[1])

Clause (1) of section 110 is generally intended to set out the conditions under which performances or displays, in the course of instructional activities other than educational broadcasting, are to be exempted from copyright control. The clause covers all types of copyrighted works, and exempts their performance or display "by instructors or pupils in the course of face-to-face teaching activities of a nonprofit educational institution," where the activities take place "in a classroom or similar place devoted to instruction."

There appears to be no need for a statutory definition of "face-to-face" teaching activities to clarify the scope of the provision. "Face-to-face teaching activities" under clause (1) embrace instructional performances and displays that are not "transmitted." The concept does not require that the teacher and students be able to see each other, although it does require their simultaneous presence in the same general place. Use of the phrase "in the course of face-to-face teaching activities" is intended to exclude broadcasting or other transmissions from an outside location into classrooms, whether radio or television and whether open or closed circuit. However, as long as the instructor and pupils are in the same building or general area, the exemption would extend to the use of devices for amplifying or reproducing sound and for projecting visual images. The "teaching activities" exempted by the clause encompass systematic instruction of a very wide variety of subjects, but they do not include performances or displays, whatever their cultural value or intellectual appeal, that are given for the recreation or entertainment of any part of their audience.

Works Affected.—Since there is no limitation on the types of works covered by the exemption, teachers or students would be free to perform or display anything in class as long as the other conditions of the clause are met. They could read aloud from copyrighted text material, act out a drama, play or sing a musical work, perform a motion picture or filmstrip, or display text or pictorial material to the class by means of a projector. However, nothing in this provision is intended to sanction the unauthorized reproduction of copies or phonorecords for the purpose of classroom performance or display, and the clause contains a special exception dealing with performances from unlawfully made copies of motion pictures and other audiovisual works, to be discussed below.

Instructors or Pupils.—To come within clause (1), the performance or display must be "by instructors or pupils," thus ruling out performances by actors, singers, or instrumentalists brought in from outside the school to put on a program. However, the term "instructors" would be broad enough to include guest lecturers if their instructional activities remain confined to classroom situations. In general, the term "pupils" refers to the enrolled members of a class.

Nonprofit Educational Institution.—Clause (1) makes clear that it applies only to the teaching activities "of a nonprofit educational institution," thus excluding from the exemption performances or displays in profit-making institutions such as dance studios and language schools.

Classroom or Similar Place.—The teaching activities exempted by the clause must take place "in a classroom or similar place devoted to instruction." For example, performances in an auditorium or stadium during a school assembly, graduation ceremony, class play, or sporting event, where the audience is not confined to the members of a particular class, would fall outside the scope of clause (1), although in some cases they might be exempted by clause (4) of section 110. The "similar place" referred to in clause (1) is a place which is "devoted to instruction" in the same way a classroom is; common examples would include a studio, a workshop, a gymnasium, a training field, a library, the stage of an auditorium, or the auditorium itself, if it is actually used as a classroom for systematic instructional activities.

Motion Pictures and Other Audiovisual Works.—The final provision of clause (1) deals with the special problem of performances from unlawfully-made copies of motion pictures and other audiovisual works. The exemption is lost where the copy being used for a classroom performance was "not lawfully made under this title" and the person responsible for the performance knew or had reason to suspect as much. This special exception to the exemption would not apply to performances from lawfully-made copies, even if the copies were acquired from someone who had stolen or converted them, or if the performances were in violation of an agreement. However, though the performance would be exempt under section 110(1) in such cases, the copyright owner might have a cause of action against the unauthorized distributor under section 106(3), or against the person responsible for the performance, for breach of contract.

Projection Devices.—As long as there is no transmission beyond the place where the copy is located, both section 109(b) and section 110(1) would permit the classroom display of a work by means of any sort of projection device or process.

DISCUSSION OF THE LAW

The face-to-face teaching exception is both narrow, in that it applies only in a very specific situation (that of teaching where students are physically in the classroom), and broad, in that it allows for the display or performance of any lawfully obtained work. This exception applies to both teachers and students such that if the entire class wishes to perform an in-copyright play in the classroom, they could all participate. Note that for this exception to apply, the school must be a nonprofit educational institution—so, a for-profit educational institution, such as the former Kaplan University, could not avail itself of this exception. However, a private university, such as Harvard, is still a nonprofit educational institution and, as such, qualifies for this exception.

The next requirement for the exception to apply is that the instruction be provided "in a classroom or similar place devoted to instruction." It is rather obvious that a university room full of enrolled students constitutes a classroom for purposes of Section 110(1). What is less clear is whether a public library space, for instance, constitutes a "similar place devoted to instruction." Reviewing the legislative history—which is quite dated, as it was written in 1976—it appears that the drafters of Section 110 would answer "maybe." They do seem to list a library as a potential location for a place devoted to instruction as long as the space is used for "systemic instructional activities." However, as you will note if you read the statute carefully, this requirement that the classroom be the location for "systemic instructional activities" never made it into the final version of the statute and, as such, is not the law as it stands. Therefore, many public librarians, when engaging in programming to teach, do consider library spaces to qualify under Section 110(1) as a "similar place devoted to instruction."

One limitation on the broad rights under Section 110(1) relating to the performance or display of any work is that this section does not permit the reproduction of the work. Thus, this is not an appropriate section of the law to consider e-reserves or the distribution of classroom materials in course-packs. Instead, for reproduction of classroom materials, consult chapter 10, "Fair Use."

Another limitation is that the work being displayed or performed, in the case of movies and other audiovisual works, must be from a lawfully obtained source. In other words, you cannot stream an illegal movie through the internet during class or take an illegal video of a movie in the movie theater to show in class. You may, however, bring in any movie that you legally own (a copy that you purchased new or used) or you can borrow a movie from the library (or even a friend) to show a movie in class.

One exception to the rule regarding the performance of a full-length movie during class is when the licensing or the contract signed by the person intending to show the movie provides that the movie may not be shown in class. In that case, like any case with a binding contractual agreement, the contractual terms will bind the user and may prevent them from showing the movie in class.

Similarly, when a large audience is invited to watch a movie on campus, the face-to-face teaching exception to copyright no longer applies. In that instance, the campus would need to purchase public performance rights in order to show the movie.

Case Study: Public Performance Rights

Recently, a public school parent-teacher association (PTA) made the news when it showed a Disney film (*The Lion King*) to raise funds for the PTA. Disney fined the PTA $250 for failing to obtain public performance rights prior to showing the film at the public event.[1] Although this created some bad press for Disney, the PTA was not showing the movie during the school day only to students and, as such, Section 110(1) of the Copyright Act did not provide the PTA with a copyright exception to paying for public performance rights.

COMMON SCENARIOS

⟳ **A professor at a nonprofit university contacts the library asking whether they can show the full-length movie *Coco* by Disney to their university classroom. The professor owns a copy of the DVD. May they show the entire movie during class?**

Yes. As long as the classroom is meeting face-to-face and the professor is using a lawful copy of the movie (one they own or one they borrowed from the library), the entire movie may be shown.

⊃ **A professor at a nonprofit university contacts the library asking whether they can show the full-length movie *Coco* by Disney to their online university class. The professor owns a copy of the DVD. May they show the entire movie during class?**

No, not under Section 110(1) of the Copyright Act, which provides for face-to-face movie performances during class. The professor would instead need to operate under the TEACH Act, or Section 110(2) of the Copyright Act, which is much more restrictive, in order to show the movie during an online class. (Note, too, that this does not involve making a copy of the movie, but rather, streaming the movie online live to the class). In the case of live online streaming, Section 110(2), or the TEACH Act, would permit the professor to show only "reasonable and limited portions" of any work when teaching online. Thus, the answer under the TEACH Act is also no, as further explained in the following chapter.

⊃ **A student group wishes to show the full-length movie *Coco* by Disney as part of a meeting. The group is making the event open to the entire university population. May they show the entire movie during their event?**

No. This is not considered a face-to-face teaching experience because it is not limited to enrolled students in a course and is available to the entire campus. In this circumstance, the student group should pay for public performance rights to show the movie.

TOOLS & RESOURCES

Band, Jonathan, Peter Jaszi, and Kenneth D. Crews. "Performance of or Showing Films in the Classroom." American Library Association. http://www.ala.org/advocacy/sites/ala.org.advocacy/files/content/copyright/fairuse/web-digital%20delivery%20in%20classroomrev3psa.pdf.

This is a discussion document providing an overview of how Section 110(1), the face-to-face copyright exception for teaching, and Section 110(2), the TEACH Act, differ when showing films for educational purposes.

"Copyright & Film Screening Best Practices." Adopted from Carla Myers, assistant librarian and coordinator of Scholarly Communication, Miami University Libraries. CC BY 4.0.

This document, appendix B of this book, is helpful when developing a local policy for when to obtain public performance rights to screen films on university campuses.

NOTE

1. Alaa Elassar, "A School Played 'The Lion King' at a Fundraising Event. Now It Has to Pay a Third of What It Raised," CNN, last updated February 6, 2020, https://www.cnn.com/2020/02/04/us/lion-king-elementary-school-250-trnd/index.html.

CHAPTER 8

The TEACH Act

Title 17, Section 110(2): Limitations on Exclusive Rights—Exemption of Certain Performances and Displays

Notwithstanding the provisions of section 106, the following are not infringements of copyright:

(1) except with respect to a work produced or marketed primarily for performance or display as part of mediated instructional activities transmitted via digital networks, or a performance or display that is given by means of a copy or phonorecord that is not lawfully made and acquired under this title, and the transmitting government body or accredited nonprofit educational institution knew or had reason to believe was not lawfully made and acquired, the performance of a nondramatic literary or musical work or reasonable and limited portions of any other work, or display of a work in an amount comparable to that which is typically displayed in the course of a live classroom session, by or in the course of a transmission, if—

   (A) the performance or display is made by, at the direction of, or under the actual supervision of an instructor as an integral part of a class session offered as a regular part of the systematic mediated instructional activities of a governmental body or an accredited nonprofit educational institution;

   (B) the performance or display is directly related and of material assistance to the teaching content of the transmission;

   (C) the transmission is made solely for, and, to the extent technologically feasible, the reception of such transmission is limited to—

      (i) students officially enrolled in the course for which the transmission is made; or

      (ii) officers or employees of governmental bodies as a part of their official duties or employment; and

   (D) the transmitting body or institution—

      (i) institutes policies regarding copyright, provides informational materials to faculty, students, and relevant staff members that accurately describe, and promote compliance with, the laws of the United States relating to copyright, and provides notice to students that materials used in connection with the course may be subject to copyright protection; and

(ii) in the case of digital transmissions—

(I) applies technological measures that reasonably prevent—

(aa) retention of the work in accessible form by recipients of the transmission from the transmitting body or institution for longer than the class session; and

(bb) unauthorized further dissemination of the work in accessible form by such recipients to others; and

(II) does not engage in conduct that could reasonably be expected to interfere with technological measures used by copyright owners to prevent such retention or unauthorized further dissemination[.]

Title 17, Section 112(f): Limitations on Exclusive Rights—Ephemeral Recordings

(1) Notwithstanding the provisions of section 106, and without limiting the application of subsection (b), it is not an infringement of copyright for a governmental body or other nonprofit educational institution entitled under section 110(2) to transmit a performance or display to make copies or phonorecords of a work that is in digital form and, solely to the extent permitted in paragraph (2), of a work that is in analog form, embodying the performance or display to be used for making transmissions authorized under section 110(2), if—

(A) such copies or phonorecords are retained and used solely by the body or institution that made them, and no further copies or phonorecords are reproduced from them, except as authorized under section 110(2); and

(B) such copies or phonorecords are used solely for transmissions authorized under section 110(2).

(2) This subsection does not authorize the conversion of print or other analog versions of works into digital formats, except that such conversion is permitted hereunder, only with respect to the amount of such works authorized to be performed or displayed under section 110(2), if—

(A) no digital version of the work is available to the institution; or

(B) the digital version of the work that is available to the institution is subject to technological protection measures that prevent its use for section 110(2).

House of Representatives, 94th Congress 2d Session, House Report No. 94-1476 (1976) (Legislative History of Section 110[2])

Instructional Broadcasting. Works Affected.—The exemption for instructional broadcasting provided by section 110(2) would apply only to "performance of a nondramatic literary or musical work or display of a work." Thus, the copyright owner's permission would be required for the performance on educational television or radio of a dramatic work, of a dramatico-musical work such as an opera or musical comedy, or of a motion picture. Since, as already explained, audiovisual works such as filmstrips are equated with motion pictures, their sequential showing would be regarded as a performance rather than a display and would not be exempt under section 110(2). The clause is not intended to limit in any way the copyright owner's exclusive right to make dramatizations, adaptations, or other derivative works under section 106(2). Thus, for example, a performer could read a nondramatic literary work aloud under section 110(2), but the copyright owner's permission would be required for him to act it out in dramatic form.

Systematic Instructional Activities.—Under section 110(2) a transmission must meet three specified conditions in order to be exempted from copyright liability. The first of these, as provided by subclause (A), is that the performance or display must be "a regular part of the systematic instructional activities of a governmental body or a nonprofit educational institution." The concept of "systematic instructional activities" is intended as the general equivalent of "curriculums," but it could be broader in a case such as that of an institution using systematic teaching methods not related to specific course work. A transmission would be a regular part of these activities if it is in accordance with the pattern of teaching established by the governmental body or institution. The use of commercial facilities, such as those of a cable service, to transmit the performance or display, would not affect the exemption as long as the actual performance or display was for nonprofit purposes.

Content of Transmission.—Subclause (B) requires that the performance or display be directly related and of material assistance to the teaching content of the transmission.

Intended Recipients.—Subclause (C) requires that the transmission is made primarily for:

(i)   Reception in classrooms or similar places normally devoted to instruction, or

(ii)   Reception by persons to whom the transmission is directed because their disabilities or other special circumstances prevent their attendance in classrooms or similar places normally devoted to instruction, or

(iii)   Reception by officers or employees of governmental bodies as a part of their official duties or employment.

In all three cases, the instructional transmission need only be made "primarily" rather than "solely" to the specified recipients to be exempt. Thus, the transmission could still be exempt even though it is capable of reception by the public at large. Conversely, it would not be regarded as made "primarily" for one of the required groups of recipients if the principal purpose behind the transmission is reception by the public at large, even if it is cast in the form of instruction and is also received in classrooms. Factors to consider in determining the "primary" purpose of a program would include its subject matter, content, and the time of its transmission.

Paragraph (i) of subclause (C) generally covers what are known as "in-school" broadcasts, whether open- or closed-circuit. The reference to "classrooms or similar places" here is intended to have the same meaning as that of the phrase as used in section 110(1). The exemption in paragraph (ii) is intended to exempt transmissions providing systematic instruction to individuals who cannot be reached in classrooms because of "their disabilities or other special circumstances." Accordingly, the exemption is confined to instructional broadcasting that is an adjunct to the actual classwork of nonprofit schools or is primarily for people who cannot be brought together in classrooms such as preschool children, displaced workers, illiterates, and shut-ins.

There has been some question as to whether or not the language in this section of the bill is intended to include instructional television college credit courses. These telecourses are aimed at undergraduate and graduate students in earnest pursuit of higher educational degrees who are unable to attend daytime classes because of daytime employment, distance from campus, or some other intervening reason. So long as these broadcasts are aimed at regularly enrolled students and conducted by recognized higher educational institutions, the committee believes that they are clearly within the language of section 110(2)(C)(ii). Like night school and correspondence courses before them, these telecourses are fast becoming a valuable adjunct of the normal college curriculum.

The third exemption in subclause (C) is intended to permit the use of copyrighted material, in accordance with the other conditions of section 110(2), in the course of instructional transmissions for Government personnel who are receiving training "as a part of their official duties or employment."

DISCUSSION OF THE LAW

The Technology, Education and Copyright Harmonization (TEACH) Act, passed in 2002, was supposed to make a copyright exception for online teaching similar to the one for the display and performance of works during face-to-face teaching provided in Section 110(1) of the Copyright Act. Unfortunately, the TEACH Act missed the mark and is not nearly as useful as it was supposed to be. In fact, many copyright librarians ignore the TEACH Act completely and proceed directly to fair use when using materials in online teaching because of the cumbersome requirements the TEACH Act includes prior to allowing the use of works for online teaching.

One thing that is different about the online-teaching exception is that the work must be "directly related and of material assistance to the teaching content" of the lesson. Under this exception, instructors are not allowed to use material to entertain students. Instructors can display any work or perform an entire "nondramatic literary or musical work" (songs, but not plays or operas), or "reasonable and limited portions" of any other work, but any work performed or displayed must be from a lawful source.

The real barriers to using the TEACH Act, though, come from the technical requirements for the display and performance of works used in online teaching. The works used in the course must be limited to the students enrolled in the course, and the educator must use reasonable technological measures to prevent students from downloading files or keeping the works after the class session ends. "The school must have copyright policies; distribute those policies to faculty, staff, and students; and notify students that material used in the course 'may be subject to copyright protection.' . . . And the school must not do anything that would likely circumvent any anti-piracy protection surrounding the works in question (so no breaking copy protection in order to show the work to the class)."[1]

COMMON SCENARIOS

⊃ **A professor wishes to share PowerPoint slides during a synchronous online class and is using copyright-protected materials as content for the slides. Can the professor successfully display the slides using the TEACH Act?**

It depends on many factors. Does the professor's university follow the many rules proscribed by the TEACH Act, such as having and distributing copyright policies to faculty staff and students? Does the professor notify students that materials used in the course may be subject to copyright protection? Does the school help limit circumvention of antipiracy protections? Does the school use technological measures on its course management system to prevent students from downloading files? I would assume, naturally, that the answer to at least some of these questions is no. If that is the case, then the professor can likely still display and distribute the slides to students, but by using a fair use analysis instead.

⊃ **A professor had been showing the full-length Disney movie *Coco* during class by playing a personal copy of a DVD appropriately under section 110(1) of the Copyright Act. Now their class has moved online. Can the professor play the movie during their online synchronous class under the TEACH Act?**

No. The TEACH Act permits showing only "reasonable and limited portions" of any work when teaching online and may not show a full-length movie. This is one of the main issues with teaching online in the digital age—sometimes it is impossible to find a licensable streaming version of a film. Of course, a professor can always use the fair use provision to stream a movie to an online class if no streaming version is available for purchase (but note that there are also issues related to breaking digital locks in order to make the copy to stream under the DMCA), and some institutions take advantage of the Academic Libraries Video Trust to access films in obsolete formats (VHS) for library use (see https://alvt .videotrust.org/).

⊃ **A librarian plans to play popular music as part of a discussion about copyright. They want to play a full-length song for members of a webinar and then play a different song that was challenged as infringing the original song's copyright as part of the discussion. The librarian has CDs of both songs and plans to play them during the online class. Does the TEACH Act permit it?**

Is the webinar the type of event contemplated by the TEACH Act? It probably depends. If this is a series of webinars offered by the library for members of the library community (students and professors), then probably so. If the target audience "enrolled" in the course, then it would likely fit within the constraints of the TEACH Act. Then, yes, the performance of an entire song is permissible under the TEACH Act, as long as the song is not part of a play or an opera, the song was lawfully acquired (the librarian or the library purchased the CD), and reasonable technological measures are used to prevent webinar students attending the webinar from downloading files or keeping the works after the session ends. If the librarian wishes to record and resubmit the recording for those who missed the webinar, they might wish to think about whether it could be justified as a fair use.

However, if the webinar is meant for a broader audience, such as the general public or a group of librarians from many different institutions, then the TEACH Act likely would not apply. In that instance, though, the librarian should think through whether the contemplated use could constitute a fair use.

TOOLS & RESOURCES

Gormley, Holland. "TEACHing from a Distance and Copyright Considerations." *Copyright: Creativity at Work* (blog), March 17, 2020. https://blogs.loc.gov/ copyright/2020/03/teaching-from-a-distance-and-copyright -considerations/.

During the COVID-19 pandemic, instructors had to rapidly shift many in-person courses online. At that time, a blog from the U.S. Copyright Office featured this post about the TEACH Act.

Louisiana State University Libraries. TEACH Act Toolkit. https://www.lib.lsu.edu/services/copyright/teach/index.

A Louisiana State University Libraries guide provides a thorough introduction to the TEACH Act, as well as checklists for libraries wishing to adopt TEACH Act policies and procedures.

Myers, Carla S. "Is the TEACH Act Enough?" In *Copyright Conversations: Rights Literacy in a Digital World,* edited by Sara R. Benson. Chicago: ACRL, 2019. Available at https://sc.lib.miamioh.edu/handle/2374.MIA/6550. CC BY-NC 4.0.

Copyright expert Carla Myers addresses the question of whether the TEACH Act is enough to cover the full range of intended uses of copyrighted works in online teaching in this open-access book chapter.

NOTE

1. Holland Gormley, "TEACHing from a Distance and Copyright Considerations," *Copyright: Creativity at Work* (blog), March 17, 2020, https://blogs.loc.gov/copyright/2020/03/teaching-from-a-distance-and-copyright-considerations/.

CHAPTER 9

Noncommercial Performance of Nondramatic Literary or Musical Works

Title 17, Section 110(4): Limitations on Exclusive Rights—
Exemption of Certain Performances and Displays

(4)   performance of a nondramatic literary or musical work otherwise than in a transmission to the public, without any purpose of direct or indirect commercial advantage and without payment of any fee or other compensation for the performance to any of its performers, promoters, or organizers, if—

 (A)   there is no direct or indirect admission charge; or

 (B)   the proceeds, after deducting the reasonable costs of producing the performance, are used exclusively for educational, religious, or charitable purposes and not for private financial gain, except where the copyright owner has served notice of objection to the performance under the following conditions:

  (i)   the notice shall be in writing and signed by the copyright owner or such owner's duly authorized agent; and

  (ii)   the notice shall be served on the person responsible for the performance at least seven days before the date of the performance, and shall state the reasons for the objection; and

  (iii)   the notice shall comply, in form, content, and manner of service, with requirements that the Register of Copyrights shall prescribe by regulation[.]

House of Representatives, 94th Congress 2d Session, House Report
No. 94-1476 (1976) (Legislative History of Section 110(4))
Certain Other Nonprofit Performances. In addition to the educational and religious exemptions provided by clauses (1) through (3) of section 110, clause (4) contains a general exception to

the exclusive right of public performance that would cover some, though not all, of the same ground as the present "for profit" limitation.

Scope of Exemption.—The exemption in clause (4) applies to the same general activities and subject matter as those covered by the "for profit" limitation today: public performances of nondramatic literary and musical works. However, the exemption would be limited to public performances given directly in the presence of an audience whether by means of living performers, the playing of phonorecords, or the operation of a receiving apparatus, and would not include a "transmission to the public." Unlike the clauses (1) through (3) and (5) of section 110, but like clauses (6) through (8), clause (4) applies only to performing rights in certain works, and does not affect the exclusive right to display a work in public.

No Profit Motive.—In addition to the other conditions specified by the clause, the performance must be "without any purpose of direct or indirect commercial advantage." This provision expressly adopts the principle established by the court decisions construing the "for profit" limitation: that public performances given or sponsored in connection with any commercial or profit-making enterprises are subject to the exclusive rights of the copyright owner even though the public is not charged for seeing or hearing the performance.

No Payment for Performance.—An important condition for this exemption is that the performance be given "without payment of any fee or other compensation for the performance to any of its performers, promoters, or organizers." The basic purpose of this requirement is to prevent the free use of copyrighted material under the guise of charity where fees or percentages are paid to performers, promoters, producers, and the like. However, the exemption would not be lost if the performers, directors, or producers of the performance, instead of being paid directly "for the performance," are paid a salary for duties encompassing the performance. Examples are performances by a school orchestra conducted by a music teacher who receives an annual salary, or by a service band whose members and conductors perform as part of their assigned duties and who receive military pay. The committee believes that performances of this type should be exempt, assuming the other conditions in clause (4) are met, and has not adopted the suggestion that the word "salary" be added to the phrase referring to the "payment of any fee or other compensation."

Admission Charge.—Assuming that the performance involves no profit motive and no one responsible for it gets paid a fee, it must still meet one of two alternative conditions to be exempt. As specified in subclauses (A) and (B) of section 110(4), these conditions are: (1) that no direct or indirect admission charge is made, or (2) that the net proceeds are "used exclusively for educational, religious, or charitable purposes and not for private financial gain."

Under the second of these conditions, a performance meeting the other conditions of clause (4) would be exempt even if an admission fee is charged, provided any amounts left "after deducting the reasonable costs of producing the performance" are used solely for bona fide educational, religious, or charitable purposes. In cases arising under this second condition and as provided in subclause (B), where there is an admission charge, the copyright owner is given an opportunity to decide whether and under what conditions the copyrighted work should be performed; otherwise, owners could be compelled to make involuntary donations to the fund-raising activities of causes to which they are opposed. The subclause would thus permit copyright owners to prevent public performances of their works under section 110(4)(B) by serving notice of objection, with the reasons therefor, at least seven days in advance.

DISCUSSION OF THE LAW

This exception to copyright law for the performance of a nondramatic literary or musical work such as reading a book (but not a play) or singing or playing a song (but not an opera) allows for educational and nonprofit organizations to do so without paying licensing if the performance is not in a "transmission to the public." In other words, if there is a live audience and no fee is charged (or any fees recovered are used for educational purposes), the performers need not pay a licensing fee for the performance of the work.

There are several nuances to take into account here. If the performance is recorded and distributed through a website, for instance, the exception would no longer apply due to the "transmission to the public." Similarly, if the performance is streamed to a larger audience than the people present at the time of the performance, the exception would no longer apply.[1]

COMMON SCENARIOS

⊃ **Can a university choir perform (sing) an in-copyright song in front of a live audience without paying for public performance rights?**

Yes, this is specifically allowed under Section 110(4) of the Copyright Act. As long as the performance is a free performance and it is not a "transmission to the public," this is allowed. Note that even though the choir conductor is likely a salaried employee of the university, this does not change the outcome, as noted in the legislative history referenced above.

⊃ **Can a university band perform (play) an in-copyright song in front of a live audience without paying for public performance rights if the performance is being recorded and distributed on YouTube?**

No. The transmission of the performance to the broader public through YouTube is considered a "transmission to the public," and, therefore, Section 110(4) does not permit the performance. (Note that without streaming the performance through the internet, this performance would otherwise be permissible under Section 110(4), as described in the scenario above.)

⊃ **Can a university choir perform (sing) an in-copyright song in front of a live audience without paying for public performance rights if a guest singer joins them and is paid a stipend for the performance?**

No. The stipend paid to the guest singer violates the terms of the Section 110(4) exception due to the "payment of any fee or other compensation for the performance to any of its performers, promoters."

TOOLS & RESOURCES

National Association for Music Education. "Copyright Law: An Introduction." https://nafme.org/my-classroom/copyright/copyright-law-an -introduction/.

This webpage provides a helpful introduction to copyright law, including Section 110(4) as it applies to the performance of copyrighted works by educators.

NOTE

1. I want to thank Kathleen DeLaurenti, the head librarian at the Peabody Institute at Johns Hopkins University's Arthur Friedheim Music Library, as well as Nazareth Pantaloni III, associate librarian at the Indiana University–Bloomington, for their input on this discussion of Section 110(4).

CHAPTER 10

Fair Use

THE LAW

Title 17, Section 107: Limitations on Exclusive Rights—Fair Use

Notwithstanding the provisions of sections 106 and 106A, the fair use of a copyrighted work, including such use by reproduction in copies or phonorecords or by any other means specified by that section, for purposes such as criticism, comment, news reporting, teaching (including multiple copies for classroom use), scholarship, or research, is not an infringement of copyright. In determining whether the use made of a work in any particular case is a fair use the factors to be considered shall include—

(1) the purpose and character of the use, including whether such use is of a commercial nature or is for nonprofit educational purposes;

(2) the nature of the copyrighted work;

(3) the amount and substantiality of the portion used in relation to the copyrighted work as a whole; and

(4) the effect of the use upon the potential market for or value of the copyrighted work.

The fact that a work is unpublished shall not itself bar a finding of fair use if such finding is made upon consideration of all the above factors.

Title 17, Section 504(c)(2): Remedies for Infringement—Damages and Profits

(c) Statutory Damages.—

(2) . . . The court shall remit statutory damages in any case where an infringer believed and had reasonable grounds for believing that his or her use of the copyrighted work was a fair use under section 107, if the infringer was: (i) an employee or agent of a nonprofit educational institution, library, or archives acting within the scope of his or her employment who, or such institution, library, or archives itself, which infringed by reproducing the work in copies or phonorecords. . . .

DISCUSSION OF THE LAW

Fair use is perhaps the greatest tool librarians have for making works available to the public (besides our Section 108 rights, of course); but it is also one of the most misunderstood sections of the Copyright Act, in my experience. Often, librarians are afraid to engage with fair use because they fear being sued or having some sort of employment repercussion for their exercise of fair use. Instead, fair use should be celebrated as a flexible limitation on the rights of copyright holders that allows librarians to make use of copyrighted works without asking for permission (and, perhaps more important, without paying fees to make appropriate use of the work).

While it is true that fair use is an affirmative defense[1]—meaning that a copyright owner can sue for infringement and the lawsuit would require an answer or result in a default judgment—librarians should feel a bit less wary when exercising fair use due to Section 504(c)(2) of the Copyright Act. Publishers and authors have much less incentive to sue a librarian exercising fair use because the ability to recover large damages is severely limited in the Copyright Act. Section 504(c)(2) provides that if a librarian had a reasonable, good faith belief that their use was a fair use, then the entity suing them cannot recover statutory damages (or the larger, up to $30,000 per work). Instead, the author or publisher would be limited to recovering an injunction and, potentially (if the librarian's fair use belief was misplaced) attorney's fees. Thus, making good-faith determinations of fair use (even if the fair use analysis is ultimately incorrect) does generally insulate librarians from large damage assessments.

The preamble to Section 107 of the Copyright Act (the fair use provision) states that "the fair use of a copyrighted work . . . for purposes such as criticism, comment, news reporting, teaching (including multiple copies for classroom use), scholarship, or research, is not an infringement of copyright." While this is just the beginning and not the end of the inquiry, it does situate the work of libraries and educators well and we can generally argue that our work fits squarely within the intended purpose of fair use. Next, however, Congress demands that we consider at least four factors. As such, you will note when reading case law that judges consider, at a minimum, these four factors. However, they may take into account other factors as well.

The first factor, the purpose and character of the use, focuses on whether the "use is of a commercial nature or is for nonprofit educational purposes." I generally like to think of these cases on a spectrum, where one side is less likely

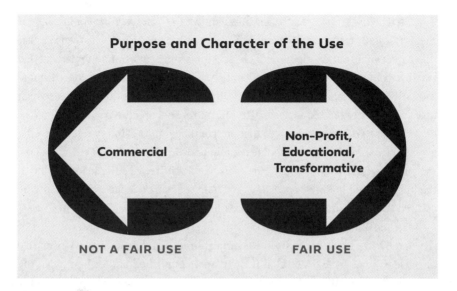

FIGURE 10.1 Purpose and Character of the Use

to be a fair use and the other is more likely to be a fair use. For this factor, then, the spectrum of use would look like figure 10.1.

As you can see from figure 10.1, the more commercial the use is, the more likely a court would consider it not to be a fair use. On the other end of the spectrum, however, are nonprofit or educational uses, which generally are considered to be a fair use purpose. Transformative uses are also considered to be fair uses. A transformative use is defined as a use that "adds something new, with a further purpose or different character, altering the [work used] with new expression, meaning, or message."[2] In contrast with a straight copying case, where the original is simply put on a copy machine for further distribution, transformative uses take the original in order to do something new and different with it. Some examples of transformative uses include parodies, using thumbnail images on the internet to index webpages, and making copies of entire books to make them searchable in "snippet" view. The Supreme Court developed the transformative use test from the "purpose and character of the use," and, as such, it is generally discussed under the first factor. Put more simply, transformative fair use can be thought of as a two-part inquiry: first, "Did the use 'transform' the material taken from the copyrighted work by using it for a broadly beneficial purpose different from that of the original, or did it just repeat the work for the same intent and value as the original?" And second, "Was the material taken appropriate in kind and amount, considering the nature of the copyrighted work and of the use?"[3] However, as

discussed below, transformative uses also impact the other factors. For instance, if the use is highly transformative, then the new work is unlikely to negatively impact the market value of the original work because it is aimed at a different market. One use that comes to mind in a library context that is likely to be considered transformative, for instance, is a library guide. The purpose of the library guide, which may contain copyrighted images, is to inform readers about a particular topic or direct them to relevant resources that are contained in the library relating to the given topic. Should the library guide contain book images—a jacket cover to show the patron what the book looks like—this would not replace the market value of the image on the book, but rather, would help the patron locate the book and be assured they have found the correct book in the library.

The nature of the copyrighted work (figure 10.2) is focused on the type of the underlying work being used for either direct copying or a transformative purpose. Courts have found that if the work is published and/or historical, the use is more likely to be a fair use, whereas if the use is unpublished or highly creative (such as poetry or fiction), it is less likely to be considered a fair use. However, the end of the statute provides that simply because the work is unpublished will "not itself bar a finding of fair use if such finding is made upon consideration of all" of the fair use factors. Lately, the courts have found this factor to be less and less useful to a fair use determination, and generally it carries little weight—especially in transformative use cases.[4] As such, this should not be significant in any fair use determination.

The inquiry under the third factor (figure 10.3) is generally understandable: how much of the underlying work did you take? Most of the time, with straight copying or scanning, taking the entire work is too much, but of course, not all the time—see second case study example below.

However, one of the more difficult concepts in understanding fair use is whether you have taken the "heart of the work" when reusing the original work. While measuring the amount taken of the work generally constitutes a quantitative analysis of the amount of the work used, the "heart of the work" factor asks whether the portion used was, qualitatively, the most important part of the work taken. While this factor will necessarily differ in each case, in at least one instance, the Supreme Court has noted that the amount taken can be quantitatively small when compared to the length of the work as a whole, but still constitute the heart of the work when the part taken is "the most interesting and moving part of the entire manuscript."[5] And yet, when the use of the work is highly transformative, taking the heart of the work may be justified when "the alleged infringer can only achieve his purpose by copying" the most important

FIGURE 10.2 Nature of the Copyrighted Work

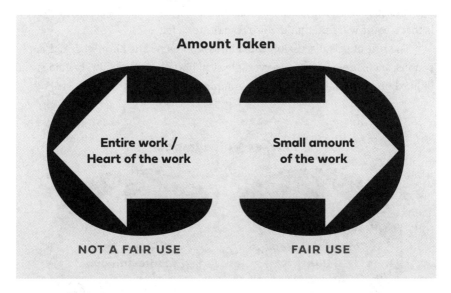

FIGURE 10.3 Amount Taken

part of the work.[6] Especially in cases where the transformative purpose is to parody the original work, the Supreme Court has noted that it is important to use the heart of the work to make fun of the original work and to permit the public to understand the comparison the parodist is trying to make.[7]

Generally, there are two distinct types of fair use assessments: (1) a typical statutory application scenario where the librarian or patron is simply making a copy of part or all of a work, and (2) a transformative use scenario, where the librarian or patron is using all or a portion of a work to make something new with a new meaning or message. Under a typical statutory application, the amount of the work used and the availability of a license for the work generally become more important factors. Similarly, courts may be more concerned with whether the work is impacting the market value of the underlying work (figure 10.4).

In a transformative fair use scenario, courts generally consider three questions:

1. Does the copyrighted material help the person make a new point?
2. Will it help the reader or viewer get their point?
3. Have they used no more than is necessary to make their point? (Is it "just right"?)[8]

And, generally, the more transformative the new work is, the more likely it is that a court will find that the use constitutes a fair use.[9]

The rest of this discussion will address more specific library fair use applications, such as electronic reserves, physical library exhibits, library guides and online library displays, and fair use as applied to library patron requests.[10]

Market-Value Impact

Replaces (or Has Potential to Replace) Market for Original Work

Little or No Market Impact

NOT A FAIR USE

FAIR USE

FIGURE 10.4 Market-Value Impact

Electronic Reserves

One of the most common scenarios for making fair use assessments for teaching is through the use of electronic reserves services. In many institutions of higher education, the library maintains the electronic reserves. In others, such as the University of Illinois at Urbana–Champaign, individual professors are responsible for determining whether a particular excerpt constitutes fair use and can be used without paying a licensing fee or receiving permission from the copyright holder for an individual course. In any event, in both instances, someone at the institution (whether it is the individual faculty member or a librarian) must make a fair use determination. The remainder of this section will address the legal issues involved in making such a determination—because, as the *Code of Best Practices in Fair Use* provides: "It is fair use to make appropriately tailored course-related content available to enrolled students via digital networks."[11]

When deciding whether a particular work may be used for electronic reserves (rather than purchasing a license or asking students to purchase the work), the fair use factors apply in a straightforward application of the four-factor test, as there is no transformative use involved. Unfortunately, there is no set amount that constitutes fair use (such as 10 percent of the work or one chapter is always fine); this is a case-by-case inquiry and, by its nature, fact dependent. For instance, one chapter of a work could be a small amount in a very long work, but it could be half of the work if the work contains only two chapters. Similarly, if the one chapter used for electronic reserves is the "heart of the work," then no matter how small the chapter may be, it could still violate fair use to take it.

Physical Library Exhibits

Physical library exhibits in cases can be a wonderful way to display some of the collections and tools the library has to offer to patrons. Often, patrons may not be aware of all the unique collections held in the library, and an exhibit case displaying key collections can increase visibility and access to valuable library assets. Of course, many of the activities performed in physical library exhibits fall under the right of first sale and do not involve fair use at all. For instance, displaying the physical copy of a book, book jacket, or other physical object itself (and not a reproduction of it) is permissible under the first sale doctrine, under Section 109(c) of the Copyright Act permitting "the owner of a particular copy . . . to display that copy publicly . . . to viewers present at the place where the copy is located." However, should the library wish to make copies of pages from a book to display in an exhibit, or quote portions of a book, or copy the dustjacket of a book for a public display, each of those activities would require a fair use analysis. Luckily, the Association of Research Libraries' *Code of Best Practices in Fair Use for Academic and Research Libraries* has already analyzed this exact scenario and provides librarians with useful advice: "It is fair use for a library to use appropriate selections from collection materials to increase public awareness and engagement with these collections and to promote new scholarship drawing on them."[12] Of course, the *Code of Best Practices* also notes that full attribution should be included and that the amount used in the display should be "appropriate to the illustrative purpose."[13]

Library Guides and Online Library Displays

The fair use analysis for library guides and online library displays is quite similar to the one for physical library displays; however, at least one part of the analysis changes. In terms of the visibility of the use and the length of the use, the fact that the work is being displayed on the open internet makes the use a bit more complicated and requires a bit more consideration. The same fair use principle applies to digital displays of library materials as it does to physical displays. Specifically, "[i]t is fair use for a library to use appropriate selections from collection materials to increase public awareness and engagement with these collections and to promote new scholarship drawing on them."[14]

Library Patrons and Fair Use

When armed with knowledge about how to apply the fair use factors to your daily work in the library, it is tempting to tell patrons whether a particular issue they face is a fair use. Please do not attempt to give legal advice to patrons. Instead, use your knowledge of fair use to provide patrons with appropriate tools, resources, and information about fair use so that the patron may make their own fair use determination. In many cases, the same tools you would access to make a fair use determination for yourself, such as the fair use checklist, would be helpful to the patron's determination as well.

Case Study: Electronic Reserves and Fair Use

In 2008, three publishers sued Georgia State University over their electronic reserves policy and processes. At the time, the reserves policy stated that up to

20 percent of a work could be copied for electronic reserves.[15] After the lawsuit began, that policy was revised to correctly note that fair use is a case-by-case analysis using a fair use checklist.[16] Indeed, the Court of Appeals for the Eleventh Circuit noted that not only does fair use require a case-by-case inquiry, but the so-called 10 percent rule is not grounded in the law and not an appropriate way to analyze fair use.[17]

This case was pending for twelve years and went back and forth numerous times between the district court and the appellate court. Throughout the course of the litigation, the district court judge consistently found that most of the electronic reserves uses by Georgia State University were fair uses. The appellate court took issue with the mechanistic nature of the district court's analysis (applying a rigid percentage weight to the fair use factors); the failure of the district court to give ample weight to the fourth fair use factor (the market harm), where the copying was nontransformative and "the threat of market substitution is significant";[18] and the district court's mistaken reevaluation of the fourth factor, which was inappropriate.[19] Ultimately, however, after the case had been pending for twelve years, the court found that the use of portions of works for electronic reserves was overwhelmingly a fair use, with the court noting that eighty-nine out of the alleged ninety-nine infringements were fair uses of the works.[20] The court (following directions from the Eleventh Circuit) gave much weight to the availability of ready licenses for the works, as this would demonstrate lost sales from creating electronic reserves copies of books. Many institutions, after this case, encourage professors to do a "market check" for available licensing before making copies of copyrighted works for electronic reserves.

Note that this case arose in the Eleventh Circuit. If your university is located in a different jurisdiction, the law may be interpreted differently—although it is highly likely that this case would be cited by the parties (and the court) with strong persuasive value.

Case Study: Text Mining and Fair Use

In 2012, the Authors Guild sued the HathiTrust Digital Library (HDL) for digitizing entire copyright-protected works to allow researchers to search for specific terms and the number of times those terms appear in the work.[21] For instance, if a researcher wished to look for a work about brain trauma, the researcher could search the phrase "brain trauma" in a copyright-protected work and the HathiTrust portal would tell them how many times that particular phrase appears in the work and on which pages. Hence, the reader could not read the book but would know whether the book was relevant to their research interests, because, after all, if the search term did not appear in that book whatsoever, the book would not be useful to their research.

The court found that this particular use of copyright protected works was "quintessentially transformative use" because "the result of a word search is different in purpose, character, expression, meaning, and message from the page (and the book) from which it is drawn. Indeed, we can discern little or no resemblance between the original text and the results of the HDL full-text search."[22] Because text searching is a fair use, the court granted summary judgment in favor of the HDL.[23]

Essentially, the court made a distinction between a consumption use of a book (for reading) and a nonconsumptive transformative use of a book (for text mining and term searching). That decision forms the basis of the justification for researchers wishing to text mine copyright-protected works for research purposes. There may, of course, be legal issues unrelated to copyright to resolve when engaging in text mining, such as concerns about potential breach of contract due to licensing or terms of service; but the copyright issues are largely resolved by the *HathiTrust* decision.

The *HathiTrust case* also served as a basis for the legal analysis in the *Google Books* case. There, instead of simply searching for a particular term inside a copyright-protected book, viewers could see the "snippet view"— a paragraph containing the highlighted search term. The court found that this, too, is a fair use (even though Google is a for-profit entity, as compared with the nonprofit digital library in *HathiTrust*) because, as with the HDL search function, Google's snippet view is transformative. The court discusses the transformative purpose in what I would call an adorable way. When discussing how Google's snippet view offers more content to the user than the HDL search terms, the court notes, for example, that

> a searcher seeking books that explore Einstein's theories, who finds that a particular book includes 39 usages of "Einstein," will nonetheless conclude she can skip that book if the snippets reveal that the book speaks of "Einstein" because that is the name of the author's cat. In contrast, the snippet will tell the searcher that this is a book she needs to obtain if the snippet shows that the author is engaging with Einstein's theories.[24]

Hence, the "snippet view . . . adds importantly to the highly transformative purpose of identifying books of interest to the searcher."[25] As such, the court affirmed the district court's grant of summary judgment in favor of Google.[26]

Case Study: Derivative Works versus Transformative Works

One area of copyright law that is particularly challenging is understanding where the line is drawn between a copyright owner's exclusive right to derivative works versus a creator's right to fair use of the original work. This concept is best explored within the context of fan fiction, where authors borrow characters and plot from preexisting works to create new, original works. Does the new work constitute a derivative, infringing on the original copyright? Or does it constitute a transformative work, justified by fair use? The answer is . . . it depends. Of course, fair use is always a case-by-case analysis, and in this circumstance, the answer is largely dependent on how different the work of fan fiction is. If the fan fiction author borrows too much of the original, the new work might be considered derivative, but if the fan fiction author gives the work a new meaning and message, it might be considered a transformative fair use.

Take, for example, the case of *Gone with the Wind* and *The Wind Done Gone*. *Gone with the Wind* is a classic work of fiction set during the Civil War in the American South and is one of the best-selling books of all time. *The Wind Done Gone* is "a critique of the depiction of slavery in *Gone with the Wind* and the Civil War–era American South."[27] I have actually read them both—and I can tell you from experience that *The Wind Done Gone* is quite a different book from *Gone with the Wind*, but I digress. The estate of *Gone with the Wind* sued the author of the new work, claiming it was an unauthorized derivative work. Originally, the district court granted the injunction and the book was not allowed to be sold.[28] On appeal to the Eleventh Circuit Court of Appeals, however, the injunction was lifted and the case was remanded for trial on the issue of whether the new book was a fair use. The appellate court found that *The Wind Done Gone* was transformative of the original work and was likely entitled to a fair use defense.[29] The court remanded the case for trial, but the parties settled out of court. Essentially, in my opinion, *The Wind Done Gone*'s author, Alice Randall, and its publisher, Houghton Mifflin, won this case. The only thing required by the settlement for them to keep selling the book was to include the label "an unauthorized parody" on the book cover and to make a donation to Morehouse College.[30]

COMMON SCENARIOS

⊃ **A professor wishes to make a copy of an entire book to put on physical reserve for students to check out and read in the library rather than placing the book itself on reserve. Can the library fulfill this request under fair use?**

While the physical book can be placed on reserve, making a copy of the book would infringe on copyright. Unless the book is in the public domain or permission is given from the publisher to make the copy, it would generally not be a fair use to copy an entire book even for an educational purpose. For a further discussion of selective lending of entire books that are still in copyright, see chapter 17, "Controlled Digital Lending."

⊃ **A professor wishes to make a copy of one chapter of a book to place on a course website for students to access. Is it a fair use to do so without paying a licensing fee or asking permission first?**

It depends. Many falsely believe that copying one chapter of a book or less than 10 percent of a book is automatically fair use. This is not true. Because fair use involves a case-by-case analysis of the circumstances, this particular use may or may not constitute fair use. The person in the best position to judge whether this particular use is a fair use is the professor making the determination. Why? The professor, better than anyone, would understand whether this chapter contains the "heart of the work." Also, how many chapters total are in the book? If this is one background chapter out of fifty, it very well may be a fair use. However, if this chapter is one of only four chapters in the entire book, it likely would not be a fair use. Another factor to consider is whether a license is available for that portion of the book. If a licensing mechanism exists, it is harder to justify fair use under the *Georgia State University* case. This would be an excellent time to point the professor toward additional fair use resources and explanations, as well as a fair use checklist, to aid in their determination. Of course, including a copyright notice on the excerpt as well as placing the excerpt on a password-protected course management system will also aid in reducing the risk of lawsuit from asserting fair use.

⊃ **A music professor is putting together a musical piece for a show choir. The professor wishes to create a "mash-up" recreation of a few copyrighted compositions put together with a new meaning and have**

the students perform it as part of their repertoire and in competitions. Is it a fair use?

Likely yes (although, of course, fair use is always case specific and different judges may interpret the law differently). There is a case with very similar facts to the hypothetical presented above. In it, a high school booster club musical director borrowed the compositions from multiple songs to create new songs for the students to sing.[31] Some of the claimants lacked standing to sue, but for the claims that were allowed to proceed, the court found that the use of the songs was a fair use.[32] Specifically, the court noted that the use of portions of the song "Magic" from *Xanadu* in a theatrical work called *Rainmaker* was a fair use because "'Rainmaker' is an entirely different theatrical work—a show piece for the high school choir that reworks pieces from multiple songs to tell a story with a new expressive content and meaning."[33]

TOOLS & RESOURCES

CODES OF BEST PRACTICES IN FAIR USE

Association of Research Libraries. *Code of Best Practices in Fair Use for Academic and Research Libraries.* Available at https://publications.arl.org/code-fair-use/.

Often, when thinking through fair use in an academic library setting, the *Code of Best Practices in Fair Use for Academic and Research Libraries* is the most helpful resource. Note that the *Code*, however, is not the law; it explains what the librarians surveyed view as appropriate fair use assessments.

Association of Research Libraries. *Code of Best Practices in Fair Use for Software Preservation.* https://www.arl.org/resources/code-of-best -practices-in-fair-use-for-software-preservation/.

Center for Media & Social Impact. *Code of Best Practices in Fair Use for Media Literacy Education.* https://cmsimpact.org/code/code-best-practices -fair-use-media-literacy-education/.

Center for Media & Social Impact. *Code of Best Practices in Fair Use for Online Video.* https://cmsimpact.org/code/code-best-practices-fair-use-online-video/.

Center for Media & Social Impact. *Code of Best Practices in Fair Use for OpenCourseWare.* 2009. https://cmsimpact.org/code/code-best -practices-fair-use-opencourseware/.

Center for Media & Social Impact. *Code of Best Practices in Fair Use for Open Educational Resources.* 2021. Available at auw.cl/oer. CC BY 4.0.

Center for Media & Social Impact. *Code of Best Practices in Fair Use for Poetry.* 2011. https://cmsimpact.org/code/code-best-practices-fair-use-poetry/.

Center for Media & Social Impact. *Code of Best Practices in Fair Use for Scholarly Research in Communication.* 2010. https://cmsimpact.org/wp-content/uploads/2016/01/WEB_ICA_CODE.pdf.

Center for Media & Social Impact. *Set of Principles in Fair Use for Journalism.* 2013. https://cmsimpact.org/wp-content/uploads/2016/01/principles_in_fair_use_for_journalism.pdf.

Center for Media & Social Impact. *Statement of Best Practices in Fair Use of Collections Containing Orphan Works for Libraries, Archives, and Other Memory Institutions.* 2014. https://cmsimpact.org/wp-content/uploads/2016/01/orphanworks-dec14.pdf.

College Art Association. *Code of Best Practices in Fair Use for Visual Arts.* https://www.collegeart.org/programs/caa-fair-use/best-practices.

ADDITIONAL RESOURCES ON COPYRIGHT

Benson, Sara R. "Fear and Fair Use: Addressing the Affective Domain." In *Copyright Conversations: Rights Literacy in a Digital World,* edited by Benson. Chicago: ACRL, 2019. http://hdl.handle.net/2142/105485. CC BY 4.0.

Discusses how fear of being sued can prevent individuals from exercising fair use rights.

Burtle, Laura. *GSU Library Copyright Lawsuit.* Georgia State University Law Library Research Guides. https://libguides.law.gsu.edu/gsucopyrightcase.

For additional information about the *Georgia State University* copyright lawsuit on electronic reserves, take a look at this library guide that includes links to all the legal decisions.

Crews, Kenneth D., and Dwayne K. Buttler. "Fair Use Checklist." Columbia University Libraries, Copyright Advisory Services, https://copyright.columbia.edu/basics/fair-use/fair-use-checklist.html.

When making a fair use assessment, the Fair Use Checklist is a very helpful tool. The checklist can be copied from this book (see appendix A) or printed from the link above and saved to document a good-faith fair use determination.

"Public Statement of Library Copyright Specialists: Fair Use & Emergency Remote Teaching & Research." March 13, 2020. https://tinyurl.com/tvnty3a.

In times of emergency like the COVID-19 pandemic, when institutions have to rapidly shift materials online, fair use is extremely helpful. A national group of copyright librarians put together this statement on fair use and emergency remote teaching and research.

Samberg, R., and C. Hennesy. "Law and Literacy in Non-Consumptive Text Mining: Guiding Researchers through the Landscape of Computational Text Analysis." In *Copyright Conversations: Rights Literacy in the Digital Age,* edited by Sara R. Benson. Chicago: ACRL, 2019. https://escholarship.org/uc/item/55j0h74g. CC BY 4.0.

Discusses why nonconsumptive text mining is a fair use.

U.S. Copyright Office. Fair Use Index, https://www.copyright.gov/fair-use/.

When looking for analogies—cases with similar situations to yours—you may consider the U.S. Copyright Office's Fair Use Index, which contains summaries of important fair use cases.

NOTES

1. See *Campbell v. Acuff-Rose Music*, 510 U.S. 569, 590 (1994).
2. *Id. at 579.*
3. Association of Research Libraries (ACRL), *Code of Best Practices in Fair Use for Academic and Research Libraries* (ACRL et al., 2012), https://publications.arl.org/code-fair-use/.
4. See *Authors Guild v. Google*, 804 F.3d 202, 220 (2d Cir. 2015).
5. *Harper & Row Publishers, Inc. v. Nation Enters.*, 471 U.S. 539, 565 (1985).
6. *Nat'l Football Scouting, Inc. v. Rang*, 912 F. Supp. 2d 985, 993 (W.D. Wa. 2012).
7. *Campbell v. Acuff-Rose Music*, 510 U.S. 569, 580 (1994).
8. Kevin Smith and Lisa Macklin, "A Framework for Analyzing any U.S. Copyright Problem" (unpublished manuscript), https://d396qusza40orc.cloudfront.net/cfel/Reading%20Docs/A%20Framework%20for%20Analyzing%20any%20Copyright%20Problem.pdf. CC BY-SA 4.0.
9. Clark D. Asay, Arielle Sloan, and Dean Sobczak, "Is Transformative Use Eating the World?" (BYU Law Research Paper No. 19-06, February 11, 2019), *61 Boston College Law Review* 905 (2020), http://dx.doi.org/10.2139/ssrn.3332682.
10. See Association of Research Libraries (ACRL), *Code of Best Practices in Fair Use for Academic and Research Libraries* (ACRL et al., 2012), 14, https://publications.arl.org/code-fair-use/.
11. *Id.* at 14.
12. *Id.*
13. *Id.* at 16.
14. *Id.* at 16.

15. *Cambridge Univ. Press v. Patton*, 769 F.3d 1232, 1242 n.8 (11th Cir. 2014).

16. *Id.* at 1242.

17. *Id.* at 1283.

18. *Id.* at 1267.

19. *Cambridge Univ. Press v. Albert*, 906 F.3d 1290, 1300 (11th Cir. 2018).

20. *Cambridge Univ. Press v. Becker*, 446 F. Supp. 3d 1145 (N.D. Ga. 2020).

21. *Authors Guild, Inc. v. HathiTrust*, 755 F.3d 87, 91 (2d Cir. 2014).

22. *Id.* at 97.

23. *Id.* at 105.

24. *Authors Guild v. Google, Inc.*, 804 F.3d 202, 218 (2d Cir. 2015).

25. *Id.*

26. *Id.* at 230.

27. *Sun Trust Bank v. Houghton Mifflin Co.*, 268 F.3d 1257, 1259 (11th Cir. 2001).

28. *Id.*

29. *Id.* at 1276.

30. The publisher made the requested revision to the book cover and continues to sell this title. "'Wind Done Gone' Copyright Case Settled," Reporters Committee for Freedom of the Press, May 29, 2002, https://www.rcfp.org/wind-done-gone-copyright-case-settled/.

31. See *Tresona Multimedia, LLC v. Burbank High School Vocal Music Ass'n*, 953 F.3d 638 (9th Cir. 2020).

32. *Id.* at 646–50.

33. *Id.* at 649.

CHAPTER 11

The Digital Millennium Copyright Act Circumvention Provisions

THE LAW

Title 17, Section 1201: Circumvention of Copyright Protection Systems

(a) Violations Regarding Circumvention of Technological Measures.—

    (1)

        (A) No person shall circumvent a technological measure that effectively controls access to a work protected under this title. . . .

        (B) The prohibition contained in subparagraph (A) shall not apply to persons who are users of a copyrighted work which is in a particular class of works, if such persons are, or are likely to be in the succeeding 3-year period, adversely affected by virtue of such prohibition in their ability to make noninfringing uses of that particular class of works under this title, as determined under subparagraph (C).

        (C) During the 2-year period described in subparagraph (A), and during each succeeding 3-year period, the Librarian of Congress, upon the recommendation of the Register of Copyrights, who shall consult with the Assistant Secretary for Communications and Information of the Department of Commerce and report and comment on his or her views in making such recommendation, shall make the determination in a rulemaking proceeding for purposes of subparagraph (B) of whether persons who are users of a copyrighted work are, or are likely to be in the succeeding 3-year period, adversely affected by the prohibition under subparagraph (A) in their ability to make noninfringing uses under this title of a particular class of copyrighted works. In conducting such rulemaking, the Librarian shall examine—

(i) the availability for use of copyrighted works;

(ii) the availability for use of works for nonprofit archival, preservation, and educational purposes;

(iii) the impact that the prohibition on the circumvention of technological measures applied to copyrighted works has on criticism, comment, news reporting, teaching, scholarship, or research;

(iv) the effect of circumvention of technological measures on the market for or value of copyrighted works; and

(v) such other factors as the Librarian considers appropriate.

(D) The Librarian shall publish any class of copyrighted works for which the Librarian has determined, pursuant to the rulemaking conducted under subparagraph (C), that noninfringing uses by persons who are users of a copyrighted work are, or are likely to be, adversely affected, and the prohibition contained in subparagraph (A) shall not apply to such users with respect to such class of works for the ensuing 3-year period.

(E) Neither the exception under subparagraph (B) from the applicability of the prohibition contained in subparagraph (A), nor any determination made in a rulemaking conducted under subparagraph (C), may be used as a defense in any action to enforce any provision of this title other than this paragraph.

. . .

(3) As used in this subsection—

(A) to "circumvent a technological measure" means to descramble a scrambled work, to decrypt an encrypted work, or otherwise to avoid, bypass, remove, deactivate, or impair a technological measure, without the authority of the copyright owner; and

(B) a technological measure "effectively controls access to a work" if the measure, in the ordinary course of its operation, requires the application of information, or a process or a treatment, with the authority of the copyright owner, to gain access to the work.

(c) Other Rights, Etc., Not Affected.—

(1) Nothing in this section shall affect rights, remedies, limitations, or defenses to copyright infringement, including fair use, under this title.

. . .

(d) Exemption for Nonprofit Libraries, Archives, and Educational Institutions.—

(1) A nonprofit library, archives, or educational institution which gains access to a commercially exploited copyrighted work solely in order to make a good faith determination of whether to acquire a copy of that work for the sole purpose of engaging in conduct permitted under this title shall not be in violation of subsection (a)(1)(A). A copy of a work to which access has been gained under this paragraph—

(A) may not be retained longer than necessary to make such good faith determination; and

(B) may not be used for any other purpose.

(2) The exemption made available under paragraph (1) shall only apply with respect to a work when an identical copy of that work is not reasonably available in another form.

(3) A nonprofit library, archives, or educational institution that willfully for the purpose of commercial advantage or financial gain violates paragraph (1)—

(A) shall, for the first offense, be subject to the civil remedies under section 1203; and

(B) shall, for repeated or subsequent offenses, in addition to the civil remedies under section 1203, forfeit the exemption provided under paragraph (1).

(4) This subsection may not be used as a defense to a claim under subsection (a)(2) or (b), nor may this subsection permit a nonprofit library, archives, or educational institution to manufacture, import, offer to the public, provide, or otherwise traffic in any technology, product, service, component, or part thereof, which circumvents a technological measure.

(5) In order for a library or archives to qualify for the exemption under this subsection, the collections of that library or archives shall be—

(A) open to the public; or

(B) available not only to researchers affiliated with the library or archives or with the institution of which it is a part, but also to other persons doing research in a specialized field.

. . .

Title 17, Section 1203: Civil Remedies

(a) Civil Actions.—Any person injured by a violation of section 1201 . . . may bring a civil action in an appropriate United States district court for such violation.

(b) Powers of the Court.—In an action brought under subsection (a), the court—

(1) may grant temporary and permanent injunctions on such terms as it deems reasonable to prevent or restrain a violation, but in no event shall impose a prior restraint on free speech or the press protected under the 1st amendment to the Constitution;

(2) at any time while an action is pending, may order the impounding, on such terms as it deems reasonable, of any device or product that is in the custody or control of the alleged violator and that the court has reasonable cause to believe was involved in a violation;

(3) may award damages under subsection (c);

(4) in its discretion may allow the recovery of costs by or against any party other than the United States or an officer thereof;

(5) in its discretion may award reasonable attorney's fees to the prevailing party; and

(6) may, as part of a final judgment or decree finding a violation, order the remedial modification or the destruction of any device or product involved in the violation that is in the custody or control of the violator or has been impounded under paragraph (2).

(c) Award of Damages.—

   (1) In general.—Except as otherwise provided in this title, a person committing a violation of section 1201 . . . is liable for either—

      (A) the actual damages and any additional profits of the violator, as provided in paragraph (2), or

      (B) statutory damages, as provided in paragraph (3).

   (2) Actual damages.—The court shall award to the complaining party the actual damages suffered by the party as a result of the violation, and any profits of the violator that are attributable to the violation and are not taken into account in computing the actual damages, if the complaining party elects such damages at any time before final judgment is entered.

   (3) Statutory damages.—

      (A) At any time before final judgment is entered, a complaining party may elect to recover an award of statutory damages for each violation of section 1201 in the sum of not less than $200 or more than $2,500 per act of circumvention, device, product, component, offer, or performance of service, as the court considers just.

. . .

   (4) Repeated violations.—In any case in which the injured party sustains the burden of proving, and the court finds, that a person has violated section 1201 . . . within 3 years after a final judgment was entered against the person for another such violation, the court may increase the award of damages up to triple the amount that would otherwise be awarded, as the court considers just.

   (5) Innocent violations.—

. . .

      (B) Nonprofit library, archives, educational institutions, or public broadcasting entities.—

. . .

         (ii) In general.—In the case of a nonprofit library, archives, [or] educational institution . . . the court shall remit damages in any case in which the library, archives, [or] educational institution . . . sustains the burden of proving, and the court finds, that the library, archives, [or] educational institution . . . was not aware and had no reason to believe that its acts constituted a violation.

37 C.F.R. Section 201.40: Exemptions to Prohibition against Circumvention

(a) *General.* This section prescribes the classes of copyrighted works for which the Librarian of Congress has determined, pursuant to 17 U.S.C. 1201(a)(1)(C) and (D), that noninfringing uses by persons who are users of such works are, or are likely to be, adversely affected. The prohibition against circumvention of technological measures that control access to copyrighted works set forth in 17 U.S.C. 1201(a)(1)(A) shall not apply to such users of the prescribed classes of copyrighted works.

(b) *Classes of copyrighted works.* Pursuant to the authority set forth in 17 U.S.C. 1201(a)(1)(C) and (D), and upon the recommendation of the Register of Copyrights, the Librarian has determined that the prohibition against circumvention of technological measures that effectively control access to copyrighted works set forth in 17 U.S.C. 1201(a)(1)(A) shall not apply to persons who engage in noninfringing uses of the following classes of copyrighted works:

   (1) Motion pictures (including television shows and videos), as defined in 17 U.S.C. 101, where the motion picture is lawfully made and acquired on a DVD protected by the Content Scramble System, on a Blu-ray disc protected by the Advanced Access Content System, or via a digital transmission protected by a technological measure, and the person engaging in circumvention under paragraph (b)(1)(i) and (b)(1)(ii) (A) and (B) of this section reasonably believes that non-circumventing alternatives are unable to produce the required level of high-quality content, or the circumvention is undertaken using screen-capture technology that appears to be offered to the public as enabling the reproduction of motion pictures after content has been lawfully acquired and decrypted, where circumvention is undertaken solely in order to make use of short portions of the motion pictures in the following instances:

      (i) For the purpose of criticism or comment:

         (A) For use in documentary filmmaking, or other films where the motion picture clip is used in parody or for its biographical or historically significant nature;

         (B) For use in noncommercial videos (including videos produced for a paid commission if the commissioning entity's use is noncommercial); or

         (C) For use in nonfiction multimedia e-books.

      (ii) For educational purposes:

         (A) By college and university faculty and students or kindergarten through twelfth-grade (K–12) educators and students (where the K–12 student is circumventing under the direct supervision of an educator), including of accredited general educational development (GED) programs, for the purpose of criticism, comment, teaching, or scholarship;

         (B) By faculty of massive open online courses (MOOCs) offered by accredited nonprofit educational institutions to officially enrolled students through online platforms (which platforms themselves may be operated for profit), in film studies or other courses requiring close analysis of film and media excerpts, for the purpose of criticism or comment, where the MOOC provider through the online platform limits transmissions to the extent technologically feasible to such officially enrolled students, institutes copyright policies and provides copyright informational materials to faculty, students, and relevant staff members, and applies technological measures that reasonably prevent unauthorized further dissemination of a work in accessible form to others or retention of the work for longer than the course session by recipients of a transmission through the platform, as contemplated by 17 U.S.C. 110(2); or

(C) By educators and participants in nonprofit digital and media literacy programs offered by libraries, museums, and other nonprofit entities with an educational mission, in the course of face-to-face instructional activities, for the purpose of criticism or comment, except that such users may only circumvent using screen-capture technology that appears to be offered to the public as enabling the reproduction of motion pictures after content has been lawfully acquired and decrypted.

(2)

(i) Motion pictures (including television shows and videos), as defined in 17 U.S.C. 101, where the motion picture is lawfully acquired on a DVD protected by the Content Scramble System, on a Blu-ray disc protected by the Advanced Access Content System, or via a digital transmission protected by a technological measure, where:

(A) Circumvention is undertaken by a disability services office or other unit of a kindergarten through twelfth-grade educational institution, college, or university engaged in and/or responsible for the provision of accessibility services to students, for the purpose of adding captions and/or audio description to a motion picture to create an accessible version as a necessary accommodation for a student or students with disabilities under an applicable disability law, such as the Americans With Disabilities Act, the Individuals with Disabilities Education Act, or Section 504 of the Rehabilitation Act;

(B) The educational institution unit in paragraph (b)(2)(i)(A) of this section has, after a reasonable effort, determined that an accessible version cannot be obtained at a fair price or in a timely manner; and

(C) The accessible versions are provided to students or educators and stored by the educational institution in a manner intended to reasonably prevent unauthorized further dissemination of a work.

(ii) For purposes of this paragraph (b)(2), "audio description" means an oral narration that provides an accurate rendering of the motion picture.

(3) Literary works, distributed electronically, that are protected by technological measures that either prevent the enabling of read-aloud functionality or interfere with screen readers or other applications or assistive technologies:

(i) When a copy of such a work is lawfully obtained by a blind or other person with a disability, as such a person is defined in 17 U.S.C. 121; provided, however, that the rights owner is remunerated, as appropriate, for the price of the mainstream copy of the work as made available to the general public through customary channels; or

(ii) When such work is a nondramatic literary work, lawfully obtained and used by an authorized entity pursuant to 17 U.S.C. 121.

. . .

(12)

    (i) Video games in the form of computer programs embodied in physical or downloaded formats that have been lawfully acquired as complete games, when the copyright owner or its authorized representative has ceased to provide access to an external computer server necessary to facilitate an authentication process to enable gameplay, solely for the purpose of:

        (A) Permitting access to the video game to allow copying and modification of the computer program to restore access to the game for personal, local gameplay on a personal computer or video game console; or

        (B) Permitting access to the video game to allow copying and modification of the computer program to restore access to the game on a personal computer or video game console when necessary to allow preservation of the game in a playable form by an eligible library, archives, or museum, where such activities are carried out without any purpose of direct or indirect commercial advantage and the video game is not distributed or made available outside of the physical premises of the eligible library, archives, or museum.

    (ii) Video games in the form of computer programs embodied in physical or downloaded formats that have been lawfully acquired as complete games, that do not require access to an external computer server for gameplay, and that are no longer reasonably available in the commercial marketplace, solely for the purpose of preservation of the game in a playable form by an eligible library, archives, or museum, where such activities are carried out without any purpose of direct or indirect commercial advantage and the video game is not distributed or made available outside of the physical premises of the eligible library, archives, or museum.

    (iii) Computer programs used to operate video game consoles solely to the extent necessary for an eligible library, archives, or museum to engage in the preservation activities described in paragraph (b)(12)(i)(B) or (b)(12)(ii) of this section.

    (iv) For purposes of this paragraph (b)(12), the following definitions shall apply:

        (A) For purposes of paragraph (b)(12)(i)(A) and (b)(12)(ii) of this section, "complete games" means video games that can be played by users without accessing or reproducing copyrightable content stored or previously stored on an external computer server.

        (B) For purposes of paragraph (b)(12)(i)(B) of this section, "complete games" means video games that meet the definition in paragraph (b)(12)(iv)(A) of this section, or that consist of both a copy of a game intended for a personal computer or video game console and a copy of the game's code that was stored or previously stored on an external computer server.

(C) "Ceased to provide access" means that the copyright owner or its authorized representative has either issued an affirmative statement indicating that external server support for the video game has ended and such support is in fact no longer available or, alternatively, server support has been discontinued for a period of at least six months; provided, however, that server support has not since been restored.

(D) "Local gameplay" means gameplay conducted on a personal computer or video game console, or locally connected personal computers or consoles, and not through an online service or facility.

(E) A library, archives, or museum is considered "eligible" when the collections of the library, archives, or museum are open to the public and/or are routinely made available to researchers who are not affiliated with the library, archives, or museum.

(13)

(i) Computer programs, except video games, that have been lawfully acquired and that are no longer reasonably available in the commercial marketplace, solely for the purpose of lawful preservation of a computer program, or of digital materials dependent upon a computer program as a condition of access, by an eligible library, archives, or museum, where such activities are carried out without any purpose of direct or indirect commercial advantage and the program is not distributed or made available outside of the physical premises of the eligible library, archives, or museum.

(ii) For purposes of the exemption in paragraph (b)(13)(i) of this section, a library, archives, or museum is considered "eligible" if—

(A) The collections of the library, archives, or museum are open to the public and/or are routinely made available to researchers who are not affiliated with the library, archives, or museum;

(B) The library, archives, or museum has a public service mission;

(C) The library, archives, or museum's trained staff or volunteers provide professional services normally associated with libraries, archives, or museums;

(D) The collections of the library, archives, or museum are composed of lawfully acquired and/or licensed materials; and

(E) The library, archives, or museum implements reasonable digital security measures as appropriate for the activities permitted by this paragraph (b)(13).

. . .

DISCUSSION OF THE LAW

There are two distinct aspects to the Digital Millennium Copyright Act (DMCA), passed in 1998. One is the provision making it illegal to break anticircumvention technology on copyrighted works, and the other is the provision for limitation of liability for internet service providers (ISPs). This chapter will cover the anticircumvention provisions; the following chapter will cover the limitation of liability for ISPs.

If you break (or circumvent) a technical lock on a DVD, for instance, and make a copy of a film without permission, you have two potential violations: one under the DMCA for breaking the technical lock and the second for copyright violation. The DMCA violation carries its own penalties, and they can be quite large, including up to $2,500 per act of circumvention if statutory damages are awarded. There is a limitation on damages for nonprofit libraries, archives, or educational institutions that can prove that they were "not aware or had no reason to believe" that their action constituted a violation.[1]

The DMCA provides that "to 'circumvent a technological measure' means to descramble a scrambled work, to decrypt an encrypted work, or otherwise to avoid, bypass, remove, deactivate, or impair a technological measure, without the authority of the copyright owner." In libraries, this most frequently might occur when a professor needs access to a film for teaching purposes but cannot simply play the film through a DVD player or VCR to the entire class (due to online teaching, for instance). The professor, then, needs to stream the video, and to do so requests that the library make a copy of the film, thereby potentially breaking the technical anticircumvention measures (or the access controls). There are, however, some exceptions provided within the text of the DMCA that are relevant to libraries—for example, a librarian can break technical locks to determine whether to purchase a copy of the work for a collection.

The DMCA also provides for the Librarian of Congress, in consultation with the Register of Copyrights, to make exemptions to the DMCA for three-year terms. Note that the Register of Copyrights, therefore, conducts a rulemaking process every three years to determine whether to extend or amend such exemptions, and is currently engaged in the eighth triennial rulemaking process for the year 2021. One such exemption is the right for K–12 and college professors to rip short clips of streaming videos that are in copyright for the purpose of teaching. Technical locks may be circumvented for short clips when the instructor reasonably believes that non-circumventing methods (such as playing a DVD in a classroom while recording a clip on a video recorder) of screen recording are insufficient to obtain the high quality necessary for teaching. There is no definition in the regulations regarding what constitutes a "short clip," but the amount is likely based on the length of clip that might otherwise constitute a fair use given the emphasis in the exemption analysis on "the impact that the prohibition on the circumvention . . . has on . . . teaching" as well as "the effect of circumvention . . . on the market for or value of copyrighted works."[2] There is also an exemption that "permits libraries, archives, and museums to break encryption when preserving and providing local access to out-of-commerce software in their collections, subject to reasonable security measures. A related rule covers preservation of video games."[3]

Current DMCA exemptions also allow circumvention of technical locks for the purpose of providing closed captions for films for students with a disability, or making an electronic work screen-reader compatible for individuals with a disability. Before making these accessible copies of videos, however, the educational institution must make a reasonable determination "that an accessible version cannot be obtained at a fair price or in a timely manner" and must take steps to "reasonably prevent" the accessible copy from being further distributed. When a disabled individual obtains a lawful copy of an electronic work with technical locks preventing the work from operating with a screen reader, that individual may circumvent the lock provided that "the rights owner is remunerated, as appropriate, for the price of the mainstream copy of the work as made available to the general public through customary channels."

Of note, "courts disagree on whether circumvention violates the DMCA when the underlying use is non-infringing (for example, because of fair use) and on what constitutes circumvention. Individual institutions will need to make their own assessments of this issue in consultation with their legal counsel or administration."[4]

COMMON SCENARIOS

⊃ **A professor wishes to show an entire movie during an online class. The movie is available through a streaming service for a fee, but they would like to make a copy of a DVD from their personal collection for streaming, using library services for both making the copy and for the streaming. Is this appropriate?**

If the movie is available for streaming through a vendor and is not in the public domain or available through Creative Commons licensing and the professor wishes to show the entire movie, the DMCA exemptions do not apply. In this case, the professor should find a source of funding (through their campus department or the library) to purchase a license to stream the movie.

⊃ **A professor wishes to show short clips of a movie during an online class. The movie is available through a streaming service for a fee, but the professor would like to use library services to make a copy of the DVD from his personal collection and make it available for streaming. Is this appropriate?**

This answer depends on whether the instructor "reasonably believes that non-circumventing alternatives are unable to produce the required level of high-quality content, or the circumvention is undertaken using screen-capture technology that appears to be offered to the public as enabling the reproduction of motion pictures after content has been lawfully acquired and decrypted." If a non-circumventing alternative, such as a playing parts of the movie on a computer and using screen-capture software, would provide suitable quality for teaching purposes, then the professor should not decrypt the DVD but use the screen-capture software. However, if the resulting clips would be too low in quality for the purposes of the professor's particular teaching purposes, then circumvention would be allowed.

⊃ **A professor wishes to show an entire movie during an online class. The movie is available through a streaming service for a fee, but the streaming version does not contain closed captioning, which the professor needs for a student with hearing impairment. The professor would like to use library services to make a copy of the DVD from his personal collection, making it available for streaming and adding closed captions specifically for the hearing-impaired student. Is this appropriate?**

Yes. The current exemptions to the DMCA permit breaking technical locks to make closed-captioned content available for students with disabilities when the movie is not available in an accessible format through a vendor for a fair price or in a timely manner and the institution takes care to provide the accessible version in a format that will not allow further distribution (so it could not, for instance, be downloaded and shared easily).

⊃ **A college professor wishes to show an entire movie during an online class. The movie is unavailable through any streaming service, and the**

professor has already requested that it be made available through a streaming service to no avail. They would like to use library services to make a copy of the DVD from their personal collection available for streaming. Is this appropriate?

This is, unfortunately, more of a gray area. Making a copy of the work in order to show it to students seems like a fair use because there is no market impact, as there is no streaming service with the available licensing. However, case law makes it unclear as to whether a fair use is justification for breaking the technical lock on the DVD. In this scenario, campus counsel might feel that making this copy is an acceptable risk, or it might not. This is an instance when connecting with campus counsel to determine the best course of action is advisable.

TOOLS & RESOURCES

Benson, Sara R. "The Copyright Implications of Teaching with Videos." Copyrightlaws.com, September 4, 2019. https://www.copyrightlaws.com/copyright-implications-teaching-with-videos/.

This article provides a description of legal issues involved when teaching using audiovisual materials protected by copyright.

U.S. Copyright Office. Eighth Triennial Rulemaking Proceedings. https://www.copyright.gov/1201/2021/.

This webpage from the Copyright Office includes the "Notice of Proposed Rulemaking" for the current exemption process, as well as the "Notice of Inquiry and Request" for petitions from the public and the public submissions to the process.

U.S. Copyright Office. "Rulemaking Proceedings under Section 1201 of Title 17." https://www.copyright.gov/1201/.

This comprehensive webpage from the Copyright Office includes short tutorials on the DMCA, links to the legal provisions of the DMCA, and links to the current exemptions to the DMCA.

NOTES

1. 17 U.S.C § 1201(c)(5)(B)(ii).
2. 17 U.S.C. § 1201(a)(1)(C).

3. Association of Research Libraries, *Code of Best Practices in Fair Use for Software Preservation* (ARL et al., 2018), appendix 2, https://www.arl.org/wp-content/uploads/2018/09/2019.2.28-software-preservation-code-revised.pdf.

4. "Public Statement of Library Copyright Specialists: Fair Use & Emergency Remote Teaching & Research," March 13, 2020, https://docs.google.com/document/d/1obaTITJbFRh7D6dH VVvfgiGP2zqaMvmoEHHZYf2cBRk/edit. Regarding courts disagreeing on the described circumvention, see *Chamberlain v. Skylink*, 381 F.3d 1178 (Fed. Cir. 2004); *MDY Industries, LLC v. Blizzard Entertainment*, 629 F.3d 928 (9th Cir. 2010); and *Universal Studios, Inc. v. Corley*, 273 F.3d 429 (2d Cir. 2001).

CHAPTER 12

The Digital Millennium Copyright Act Notice and Takedown Provisions

THE LAW

Title 17, Section 512: Limitations on Liability Relating to Materials Online

(a) Transitory Digital Network Communications.—A service provider shall not be liable for monetary relief, or, except as provided in subsection (j), for injunctive or other equitable relief, for infringement of copyright by reason of the provider's transmitting, routing, or providing connections for, material through a system or network controlled or operated by or for the service provider, or by reason of the intermediate and transient storage of that material in the course of such transmitting, routing, or providing connections, if—

(1) the transmission of the material was initiated by or at the direction of a person other than the service provider;

(2) the transmission, routing, provision of connections, or storage is carried out through an automatic technical process without selection of the material by the service provider;

(3) the service provider does not select the recipients of the material except as an automatic response to the request of another person;

(4) no copy of the material made by the service provider in the course of such intermediate or transient storage is maintained on the system or network in a manner ordinarily accessible to anyone other than anticipated recipients, and no such copy is maintained on the system or network in a manner ordinarily accessible to such anticipated recipients for a longer period than is reasonably necessary for the transmission, routing, or provision of connections; and

(5) the material is transmitted through the system or network without modification of its content.

(b) System Caching.—

    (1) Limitation on liability.—A service provider shall not be liable for monetary relief, or, except as provided in subsection (j), for injunctive or other equitable relief, for infringement of copyright by reason of the intermediate and temporary storage of material on a system or network controlled or operated by or for the service provider in a case in which—

        (A) the material is made available online by a person other than the service provider;

        (B) the material is transmitted from the person described in subparagraph (A) through the system or network to a person other than the person described in subparagraph (A) at the direction of that other person; and

        (C) the storage is carried out through an automatic technical process for the purpose of making the material available to users of the system or network who, after the material is transmitted as described in subparagraph (B), request access to the material from the person described in subparagraph (A), if the conditions set forth in paragraph (2) are met.

    (2) Conditions.—The conditions referred to in paragraph (1) are that—

        (A) the material described in paragraph (1) is transmitted to the subsequent users described in paragraph (1)(C) without modification to its content from the manner in which the material was transmitted from the person described in paragraph (1)(A);

        (B) the service provider described in paragraph (1) complies with rules concerning the refreshing, reloading, or other updating of the material when specified by the person making the material available online in accordance with a generally accepted industry standard data communications protocol for the system or network through which that person makes the material available, except that this subparagraph applies only if those rules are not used by the person described in paragraph (1)(A) to prevent or unreasonably impair the intermediate storage to which this subsection applies;

        (C) the service provider does not interfere with the ability of technology associated with the material to return to the person described in paragraph (1)(A) the information that would have been available to that person if the material had been obtained by the subsequent users described in paragraph (1)(C) directly from that person, except that this subparagraph applies only if that technology—

            (i) does not significantly interfere with the performance of the provider's system or network or with the intermediate storage of the material;

            (ii) is consistent with generally accepted industry standard communications protocols; and

            (iii) does not extract information from the provider's system or network other than the information that would have been available to the person described in paragraph (1)(A) if the subsequent users had gained access to the material directly from that person;

(D) if the person described in paragraph (1)(A) has in effect a condition that a person must meet prior to having access to the material, such as a condition based on payment of a fee or provision of a password or other information, the service provider permits access to the stored material in significant part only to users of its system or network that have met those conditions and only in accordance with those conditions; and

(E) if the person described in paragraph (1)(A) makes that material available online without the authorization of the copyright owner of the material, the service provider responds expeditiously to remove, or disable access to, the material that is claimed to be infringing upon notification of claimed infringement as described in subsection (c)(3), except that this subparagraph applies only if—

(i) the material has previously been removed from the originating site or access to it has been disabled, or a court has ordered that the material be removed from the originating site or that access to the material on the originating site be disabled; and

(ii) the party giving the notification includes in the notification a statement confirming that the material has been removed from the originating site or access to it has been disabled or that a court has ordered that the material be removed from the originating site or that access to the material on the originating site be disabled.

(c) Information Residing on Systems or Networks At Direction of Users.—

(1) In general.—A service provider shall not be liable for monetary relief, or, except as provided in subsection (j), for injunctive or other equitable relief, for infringement of copyright by reason of the storage at the direction of a user of material that resides on a system or network controlled or operated by or for the service provider, if the service provider—

(A)

(i) does not have actual knowledge that the material or an activity using the material on the system or network is infringing;

(ii) in the absence of such actual knowledge, is not aware of facts or circumstances from which infringing activity is apparent; or

(iii) upon obtaining such knowledge or awareness, acts expeditiously to remove, or disable access to, the material;

(B) does not receive a financial benefit directly attributable to the infringing activity, in a case in which the service provider has the right and ability to control such activity; and

(C) upon notification of claimed infringement as described in paragraph (3), responds expeditiously to remove, or disable access to, the material that is claimed to be infringing or to be the subject of infringing activity.

(2) Designated agent.—The limitations on liability established in this subsection apply to a service provider only if the service provider has designated an agent to receive notifications of claimed infringement described in paragraph (3), by making available through its service, including on its website in a location accessible to the public, and by providing to the Copyright Office, substantially the following information:

(A) the name, address, phone number, and electronic mail address of the agent.

(B) other contact information which the Register of Copyrights may deem appropriate.

The Register of Copyrights shall maintain a current directory of agents available to the public for inspection, including through the Internet, and may require payment of a fee by service providers to cover the costs of maintaining the directory.

(3) Elements of notification.—

(A) To be effective under this subsection, a notification of claimed infringement must be a written communication provided to the designated agent of a service provider that includes substantially the following:

(i) A physical or electronic signature of a person authorized to act on behalf of the owner of an exclusive right that is allegedly infringed.

(ii) Identification of the copyrighted work claimed to have been infringed, or, if multiple copyrighted works at a single online site are covered by a single notification, a representative list of such works at that site.

(iii) Identification of the material that is claimed to be infringing or to be the subject of infringing activity and that is to be removed or access to which is to be disabled, and information reasonably sufficient to permit the service provider to locate the material.

(iv) Information reasonably sufficient to permit the service provider to contact the complaining party, such as an address, telephone number, and, if available, an electronic mail address at which the complaining party may be contacted.

(v) A statement that the complaining party has a good faith belief that use of the material in the manner complained of is not authorized by the copyright owner, its agent, or the law.

(vi) A statement that the information in the notification is accurate, and under penalty of perjury, that the complaining party is authorized to act on behalf of the owner of an exclusive right that is allegedly infringed.

(B)

(i) Subject to clause (ii), a notification from a copyright owner or from a person authorized to act on behalf of the copyright owner that fails to comply substantially with the provisions of subparagraph (A) shall not be considered under paragraph (1)(A) in determining whether a service provider has actual knowledge or is aware of facts or circumstances from which infringing activity is apparent.

(ii) In a case in which the notification that is provided to the service provider's designated agent fails to comply substantially with all the provisions of subparagraph (A) but substantially complies with clauses (ii), (iii), and (iv) of subparagraph (A), clause (i) of this subparagraph applies only if the service provider promptly attempts to contact the person making the notification or takes other reasonable steps to assist in the receipt of notification that substantially complies with all the provisions of subparagraph (A).

(d) Information Location Tools.—A service provider shall not be liable for monetary relief, or, except as provided in subsection (j), for injunctive or other equitable relief, for infringement of copyright by reason of the provider referring or linking users to an online location containing infringing material or infringing activity, by using information location tools, including a directory, index, reference, pointer, or hypertext link, if the service provider—

(1)

(A) does not have actual knowledge that the material or activity is infringing;

(B) in the absence of such actual knowledge, is not aware of facts or circumstances from which infringing activity is apparent; or

(C) upon obtaining such knowledge or awareness, acts expeditiously to remove, or disable access to, the material;

(2) does not receive a financial benefit directly attributable to the infringing activity, in a case in which the service provider has the right and ability to control such activity; and

(3) upon notification of claimed infringement as described in subsection (c)(3), responds expeditiously to remove, or disable access to, the material that is claimed to be infringing or to be the subject of infringing activity, except that, for purposes of this paragraph, the information described in subsection (c)(3)(A)(iii) shall be identification of the reference or link, to material or activity claimed to be infringing, that is to be removed or access to which is to be disabled, and information reasonably sufficient to permit the service provider to locate that reference or link.

(e) Limitation on Liability of Nonprofit Educational Institutions.—

(1) When a public or other nonprofit institution of higher education is a service provider, and when a faculty member or graduate student who is an employee of such institution is performing a teaching or research function, for the purposes of subsections (a) and (b) such faculty member or graduate student shall be considered to be a person other than the institution, and for the purposes of subsections (c) and (d) such faculty member's or graduate student's knowledge or awareness of his or her infringing activities shall not be attributed to the institution, if—

(A) such faculty member's or graduate student's infringing activities do not involve the provision of online access to instructional materials that are or were required or recommended, within the preceding 3-year period, for a course taught at the institution by such faculty member or graduate student;

(B) the institution has not, within the preceding 3-year period, received more than two notifications described in subsection (c)(3) of claimed infringement by such faculty member or graduate student, and such notifications of claimed infringement were not actionable under subsection (f); and

(C) the institution provides to all users of its system or network informational materials that accurately describe, and promote compliance with, the laws of the United States relating to copyright.

(2) For the purposes of this subsection, the limitations on injunctive relief contained in subsections (j)(2) and (j)(3), but not those in (j)(1), shall apply.

(f) Misrepresentations.—Any person who knowingly materially misrepresents under this section—

(1) that material or activity is infringing, or

(2) that material or activity was removed or disabled by mistake or misidentification, shall be liable for any damages, including costs and attorneys' fees, incurred by the alleged infringer, by any copyright owner or copyright owner's authorized licensee, or by a service provider, who is injured by such misrepresentation, as the result of the service provider relying upon such misrepresentation in removing or disabling access to the material or activity claimed to be infringing, or in replacing the removed material or ceasing to disable access to it.

(g) Replacement of Removed or Disabled Material and Limitation on Other Liability.—

(1) No liability for taking down generally.—Subject to paragraph (2), a service provider shall not be liable to any person for any claim based on the service provider's good faith disabling of access to, or removal of, material or activity claimed to be infringing or based on facts or circumstances from which infringing activity is apparent, regardless of whether the material or activity is ultimately determined to be infringing.

(2) Exception.—Paragraph (1) shall not apply with respect to material residing at the direction of a subscriber of the service provider on a system or network controlled or operated by or for the service provider that is removed, or to which access is disabled by the service provider, pursuant to a notice provided under subsection (c)(1)(C), unless the service provider—

(A) takes reasonable steps promptly to notify the subscriber that it has removed or disabled access to the material;

(B) upon receipt of a counter notification described in paragraph (3), promptly provides the person who provided the notification under subsection (c)(1)(C) with a copy of the counter notification, and informs that person that it will replace the removed material or cease disabling access to it in 10 business days; and

(C) replaces the removed material and ceases disabling access to it not less than 10, nor more than 14, business days following receipt of the counter notice, unless its designated agent first receives notice from the person who submitted the notification under subsection (c)(1)(C) that such person has filed an action seeking a court order to restrain the subscriber from engaging in infringing activity relating to the material on the service provider's system or network.

(3) Contents of counter notification.—To be effective under this subsection, a counter notification must be a written communication provided to the service provider's designated agent that includes substantially the following:

(A) A physical or electronic signature of the subscriber.

(B) Identification of the material that has been removed or to which access has been disabled and the location at which the material appeared before it was removed or access to it was disabled.

(C) A statement under penalty of perjury that the subscriber has a good faith belief that the material was removed or disabled as a result of mistake or misidentification of the material to be removed or disabled.

(D) The subscriber's name, address, and telephone number, and a statement that the subscriber consents to the jurisdiction of Federal District Court for the judicial district in which the address is located, or if the subscriber's address is outside of the United States, for any judicial district in which the service provider may be found, and that the subscriber will accept service of process from the person who provided notification under subsection (c)(1)(C) or an agent of such person.

(4) Limitation on other liability.—A service provider's compliance with paragraph (2) shall not subject the service provider to liability for copyright infringement with respect to the material identified in the notice provided under subsection (c)(1)(C).

. . .

(i) Conditions for Eligibility.—

(1) Accommodation of technology.—The limitations on liability established by this section shall apply to a service provider only if the service provider—

(A) has adopted and reasonably implemented, and informs subscribers and account holders of the service provider's system or network of, a policy that provides for the termination in appropriate circumstances of subscribers and account holders of the service provider's system or network who are repeat infringers; and

(B) accommodates and does not interfere with standard technical measures.

(2) Definition.—As used in this subsection, the term "standard technical measures" means technical measures that are used by copyright owners to identify or protect copyrighted works and—

(A) have been developed pursuant to a broad consensus of copyright owners and service providers in an open, fair, voluntary, multi-industry standards process;

(B) are available to any person on reasonable and nondiscriminatory terms; and

(C) do not impose substantial costs on service providers or substantial burdens on their systems or networks.

(j)   Injunctions.—The following rules shall apply in the case of any application for an injunction under section 502 against a service provider that is not subject to monetary remedies under this section:

(1)   Scope of relief.—

(A) With respect to conduct other than that which qualifies for the limitation on remedies set forth in subsection (a), the court may grant injunctive relief with respect to a service provider only in one or more of the following forms:

(i)   An order restraining the service provider from providing access to infringing material or activity residing at a particular online site on the provider's system or network.

(ii) An order restraining the service provider from providing access to a subscriber or account holder of the service provider's system or network who is engaging in infringing activity and is identified in the order, by terminating the accounts of the subscriber or account holder that are specified in the order.

(iii) Such other injunctive relief as the court may consider necessary to prevent or restrain infringement of copyrighted material specified in the order of the court at a particular online location, if such relief is the least burdensome to the service provider among the forms of relief comparably effective for that purpose.

(B) If the service provider qualifies for the limitation on remedies described in subsection (a), the court may only grant injunctive relief in one or both of the following forms:

(i)   An order restraining the service provider from providing access to a subscriber or account holder of the service provider's system or network who is using the provider's service to engage in infringing activity and is identified in the order, by terminating the accounts of the subscriber or account holder that are specified in the order.

(ii) An order restraining the service provider from providing access, by taking reasonable steps specified in the order to block access, to a specific, identified, online location outside the United States.

(2)   Considerations.—The court, in considering the relevant criteria for injunctive relief under applicable law, shall consider—

(A) whether such an injunction, either alone or in combination with other such injunctions issued against the same service provider under this subsection, would significantly burden either the provider or the operation of the provider's system or network;

(B) the magnitude of the harm likely to be suffered by the copyright owner in the digital network environment if steps are not taken to prevent or restrain the infringement;

(C) whether implementation of such an injunction would be technically feasible and effective, and would not interfere with access to noninfringing material at other online locations; and

(D) whether other less burdensome and comparably effective means of preventing or restraining access to the infringing material are available.

(3) Notice and ex parte orders.—Injunctive relief under this subsection shall be available only after notice to the service provider and an opportunity for the service provider to appear are provided, except for orders ensuring the preservation of evidence or other orders having no material adverse effect on the operation of the service provider's communications network.

(k) Definitions.—

(1) Service provider.—

(A) As used in subsection (a), the term "service provider" means an entity offering the transmission, routing, or providing of connections for digital online communications, between or among points specified by a user, of material of the user's choosing, without modification to the content of the material as sent or received.

(B) As used in this section, other than subsection (a), the term "service provider" means a provider of online services or network access, or the operator of facilities therefor, and includes an entity described in subparagraph (A).

(2) Monetary relief.—As used in this section, the term "monetary relief" means damages, costs, attorneys' fees, and any other form of monetary payment.

(l) Other Defenses Not Affected.—The failure of a service provider's conduct to qualify for limitation of liability under this section shall not bear adversely upon the consideration of a defense by the service provider that the service provider's conduct is not infringing under this title or any other defense.

...

DISCUSSION OF THE LAW

The DMCA provides a limitation on damages to internet service providers. Through a system requiring an ISP to respond to takedown notices from copyright owners, an ISP can limit liability for any infringing material on its websites.

Why, you may ask, is this being discussed in a handbook on copyright for librarians? You may need to list your institution or library in the United States Copyright Office's registry of Designated Agents and, as such, you may need to respond to takedown notices from copyright owners. "To designate an agent, a service provider must do two things: (1) make certain contact information for the agent available to the public on its website; and (2) provide the same information to the Copyright Office, which maintains a centralized online directory of designated agent contact information for public use. The service provider must also ensure that this information is up to date."[1] In any event, many individuals send takedown notices even though the DMCA does not technically apply, and it behooves the responding organization to respond appropriately to the notices—the DMCA provides a framework for such an appropriate response.

Under the DMCA, an internet service provider is "an entity offering the transmission, routing, or providing of connections for digital online communications, between or among points specified by a user, of material of the user's choosing, without modification to the content of the material as sent or received." The internet site must be one where users can post content without the control of the institution. For instance, YouTube is a classic example of an ISP under the DMCA, as members of the public can post videos without modification from YouTube. Note that the DMCA specifically addresses a limitation of liability for certain instruction taking place in nonprofit educational institutions where the educational institution is considered an ISP. The university is not liable for actions taken by a faculty member or graduate student when the instructor's infringing activity generally does not relate to required or recommended online course materials within the past three years; when the institution has not received more than two notifications of claimed infringement relating to the instructor in the past three years; and when the institution instructs all ISP users in its system to comply with U.S. copyright law.

More generally, for an ISP to avoid damages for infringing material posted online by a user of its ISP, it must "not have actual knowledge that the material or an activity using the material on the system or network is infringing," and must not be "aware of facts or circumstances from which infringing activity is apparent"; and when the ISP learns of such infringing activity, it must act "expeditiously to remove, or disable access to, the material."

The general procedure for DMCA notifications as provided in the act is for a copyright owner to send a takedown notice to the designated DMCA agent.[2] The designated agent will alert the user who posted the allegedly infringing material and take it down from the website. If the user believes the work should remain online because it was removed in error or was posted under an assertion of fair use, the user will respond with a counternotice. The ISP will then provide the counternotice to the copyright owner and the work will be restored online within ten to fourteen days unless legal action is taken.[3] The Ninth Circuit Court of Appeals notes that those filing takedown notices should first do their own fair use assessment, so as not to file frivolous takedown notice requests.[4]

COMMON SCENARIOS

⊃ **A librarian has posted a copyrighted picture as part of a digital exhibit explaining the life of a famous writer. The university received a takedown notice from the photographer who took the photo of the writer demanding that the picture be removed. How should the university respond?**

First, the fact that a takedown notice was sent rather than a lawsuit demand letter is a good thing. This means the university is being treated like an ISP by the complainant and should respond within the context of the DMCA provisions, which provide some level of protection from liability. It is appropriate to respond within ten to fourteen days with a clarification that the picture in the digital exhibit is being displayed pursuant to fair use. Often, such digital exhibits commenting on specific works in the library collection would be considered fair use and the university could cite the ACRL's *Code of Best Practices for Academic and Research Libraries* for support.[5] If the university does not believe the use is a fair use, it could choose to remove the picture from the digital exhibit immediately.

⊃ **A faculty member posted a copyright-protected article to a public-facing course webpage. The university received a takedown notice demanding that the article be removed. How should the university respond?**

In this scenario, the faculty member has likely violated the terms of licensing that the library has negotiated with the publisher of the journal. Normally, library patrons are free to view and download a copy of journal articles the library subscribes to for personal or educational use. However, they are not permitted to publicly distribute the articles. Thus, the university should let the faculty member know that the article will be removed and explain the licensing terms to the faculty member so this does not occur again.

⊃ **A faculty member has a blog on a campus website. The blog post for this week features an embedded YouTube video that the faculty member found (but which was uploaded to YouTube by a third party). The university receives a takedown notice for the YouTube video. How should the university respond?**[6]

Embedding a YouTube video is essentially the same thing as linking to the video because if the video is removed from YouTube, the embedded video will not play. As such, the copyright owner really should aim their notice at the person who uploaded the video to YouTube. Embedding, or inline linking, would be considered legal if a court applies the "server test" developed in the Ninth Circuit *Perfect 10, Inc. v. Amazon.com, Inc.* case: "Providing . . . HTML instructions is not equivalent to showing a copy."[7] Additionally, "the Ninth Circuit's reasoning in *Perfect 10* has been relied on to bar direct infringement claims for instances of inline linking and framing."[8] Thus, the university could respond that it is not making a copy or violating the display rights of the copyright owner citing the *Perfect 10* decision. If there is a fair use argument to be made, that could be raised in response. Of course, the university could always agree to take down the embedded video to avoid any potential contributory liability.[9] Further, if the university is a public institution, they may not be as concerned about potential damages due to sovereign immunity, addressed in chapter 15, "Sovereign Immunity."

TOOLS & RESOURCES

U.S. Copyright Office. DMCA. https://www.copyright.gov/dmca/.

> This website is dedicated to explaining the Digital Millennium Copyright Act of 1998.

U.S. Copyright Office. DMCA Agent Registry and Frequently Asked Questions. https://www.copyright.gov/dmca-directory/faq.html.

> The DMCA Agent Registry, along with a helpful list of frequently asked questions.

NOTES

1. U.S. Copyright Office, DMCA Designated Agent Directory, https://www.copyright.gov/dmca-directory/.
2. See 17 U.S.C. § 512(c)(3).
3. *Id.* at § 512(g)(2)–(3).
4. *Lenz v. Universal Music Corp.*, 801 F.3d 1126 (9th Cir. 2015).
5. See Association of Research Libraries, *Code of Best Practices in Fair Use for Academic and Research Libraries* (ACRL et al., 2012), https://publications.arl.org/code-fair-use/.
6. I want to thank Douglas Shontz, university counsel at the University of Illinois, for helping me brainstorm potential DMCA questions.
7. 508 F.3d 1146 (9th Cir. 2007), 1161.
8. U.S. Copyright Office, *The Making Available Right in the United States: A Report of the Register of Copyrights* (2016), 49 (citations omitted), https://www.copyright.gov/docs/making_available/making-available-right.pdf.
9. *Id.* at 49n241.

CHAPTER 13

Select International Copyright Library Issues

Title 17, Section 104: National Origin

(a) Unpublished Works.—The works specified by sections 102 and 103, while unpublished, are subject to protection under this title without regard to the nationality or domicile of the author.

(b) Published Works.—The works specified by sections 102 and 103, when published, are subject to protection under this title if—

    (1) on the date of first publication, one or more of the authors is a national or domiciliary of the United States, or is a national, domiciliary, or sovereign authority of a treaty party, or is a stateless person, wherever that person may be domiciled; or

    (2) the work is first published in the United States or in a foreign nation that, on the date of first publication, is a treaty party;

. . .

        For purposes of paragraph (2), a work that is published in the United States or a treaty party within 30 days after publication in a foreign nation that is not a treaty party shall be considered to be first published in the United States or such treaty party, as the case may be.

(c) Effect of Berne Convention.—No right or interest in a work eligible for protection under this title may be claimed by virtue of, or in reliance upon, the provisions of the Berne Convention, or the adherence of the United States thereto. Any rights in a work eligible for protection under this title that derive from this title, other Federal or State statutes, or the common law, shall not be expanded or reduced by virtue of, or in reliance upon, the provisions of the Berne Convention, or the adherence of the United States thereto.

. . .

Title 17, Section 104A: Copyright in Restored Works

(a)   Automatic Protection and Term.—

  (1)   Term.—

   (A)   Copyright subsists, in accordance with this section, in restored works, and vests automatically on the date of restoration.

   (B)   Any work in which copyright is restored under this section shall subsist for the remainder of the term of copyright that the work would have otherwise been granted in the United States if the work never entered the public domain in the United States.

  (2)   Exception.—Any work in which the copyright was ever owned or administered by the Alien Property Custodian and in which the restored copyright would be owned by a government or instrumentality thereof, is not a restored work.

(b)   Ownership of Restored Copyright.—A restored work vests initially in the author or initial rightholder of the work as determined by the law of the source country of the work.

(c)   Filing of Notice of Intent to Enforce Restored Copyright Against Reliance Parties.—On or after the date of restoration, any person who owns a copyright in a restored work or an exclusive right therein may file with the Copyright Office a notice of intent to enforce that person's copyright or exclusive right or may serve such a notice directly on a reliance party. Acceptance of a notice by the Copyright Office is effective as to any reliance parties but shall not create a presumption of the validity of any of the facts stated therein. Service on a reliance party is effective as to that reliance party and any other reliance parties with actual knowledge of such service and of the contents of that notice.

. . .

(e)   Notices of Intent To Enforce a Restored Copyright.—

  (1)   Notices of intent filed with the copyright office.—

   (A)

     (i)   A notice of intent filed with the Copyright Office to enforce a restored copyright shall be signed by the owner of the restored copyright or the owner of an exclusive right therein, who files the notice under subsection (d)(2)(A)(i) (hereafter in this paragraph referred to as the "owner"), or by the owner's agent, shall identify the title of the restored work, and shall include an English translation of the title and any other alternative titles known to the owner by which the restored work may be identified, and an address and telephone number at which the owner may be contacted. If the notice is signed by an agent, the agency relationship must have been constituted in a writing signed by the owner before the filing of the notice. The Copyright Office may specifically require in regulations other information to be included in the notice, but failure to provide such other information shall not invalidate the notice or be a basis for refusal to list the restored work in the Federal Register.

(ii)   If a work in which copyright is restored has no formal title, it shall be described in the notice of intent in detail sufficient to identify it.

(iii)   Minor errors or omissions may be corrected by further notice at any time after the notice of intent is filed. Notices of corrections for such minor errors or omissions shall be accepted after the period established in subsection (d)(2)(A)(i). Notices shall be published in the Federal Register pursuant to subparagraph (B).

(B)

(i)   The Register of Copyrights shall publish in the Federal Register, commencing not later than 4 months after the date of restoration for a particular nation and every 4 months thereafter for a period of 2 years, lists identifying restored works and the ownership thereof if a notice of intent to enforce a restored copyright has been filed.

(ii)   Not less than 1 list containing all notices of intent to enforce shall be maintained in the Public Information Office of the Copyright Office and shall be available for public inspection and copying during regular business hours pursuant to sections 705 and 708.

(C)   The Register of Copyrights is authorized to fix reasonable fees based on the costs of receipt, processing, recording, and publication of notices of intent to enforce a restored copyright and corrections thereto.

(D)

(i)   Not later than 90 days before the date the Agreement on Trade-Related Aspects of Intellectual Property referred to in section 101(d)(15) of the Uruguay Round Agreements Act enters into force with respect to the United States, the Copyright Office shall issue and publish in the Federal Register regulations governing the filing under this subsection of notices of intent to enforce a restored copyright.

(ii)   Such regulations shall permit owners of restored copyrights to file simultaneously for registration of the restored copyright.

(2)   Notices of intent served on a reliance party.—

(A)   Notices of intent to enforce a restored copyright may be served on a reliance party at any time after the date of restoration of the restored copyright.

(B)   Notices of intent to enforce a restored copyright served on a reliance party shall be signed by the owner or the owner's agent, shall identify the restored work and the work in which the restored work is used, if any, in detail sufficient to identify them, and shall include an English translation of the title, any other alternative titles known to the owner by which the work may be identified, the use or uses to which the owner objects, and an address and telephone number at which the reliance party may contact the owner. If the notice is signed by an agent, the agency relationship must have been constituted in writing and signed by the owner before service of the notice.

. . .

(h) Definitions.—For purposes of this section and section 109(a):

(1) The term "date of adherence or proclamation" means the earlier of the date on which a foreign nation which, as of the date the WTO Agreement enters into force with respect to the United States, is not a nation adhering to the Berne Convention or a WTO member country, becomes—

   (A) a nation adhering to the Berne Convention;

   (B) a WTO member country;

   (C) a nation adhering to the WIPO Copyright Treaty;

   (D) a nation adhering to the WIPO Performances and Phonograms Treaty; or

   (E) subject to a Presidential proclamation under subsection (g).

(2) The "date of restoration" of a restored copyright is—

   (A) January 1, 1996, if the source country of the restored work is a nation adhering to the Berne Convention or a WTO member country on such date, or

   (B) the date of adherence or proclamation, in the case of any other source country of the restored work.

(3) The term "eligible country" means a nation, other than the United States, that—

   (A) becomes a WTO member country after the date of the enactment of the Uruguay Round Agreements Act;

   (B) on such date of enactment is, or after such date of enactment becomes, a nation adhering to the Berne Convention;

   (C) adheres to the WIPO Copyright Treaty;

   (D) adheres to the WIPO Performances and Phonograms Treaty; or

   (E) after such date of enactment becomes subject to a proclamation under subsection (g).

(4) The term "reliance party" means any person who—

   (A) with respect to a particular work, engages in acts, before the source country of that work becomes an eligible country, which would have violated section 106 if the restored work had been subject to copyright protection, and who, after the source country becomes an eligible country, continues to engage in such acts;

   (B) before the source country of a particular work becomes an eligible country, makes or acquires 1 or more copies or phonorecords of that work; or

   (C) as the result of the sale or other disposition of a derivative work covered under subsection (d)(3), or significant assets of a person described in subparagraph (A) or (B), is a successor, assignee, or licensee of that person.

(5) The term "restored copyright" means copyright in a restored work under this section.

(6)   The term "restored work" means an original work of authorship that—

    (A)   is protected under subsection (a);

    (B)   is not in the public domain in its source country through expiration of term of protection;

    (C)   is in the public domain in the United States due to—

        (i)   noncompliance with formalities imposed at any time by United States copyright law, including failure of renewal, lack of proper notice, or failure to comply with any manufacturing requirements;

        (ii)   lack of subject matter protection in the case of sound recordings fixed before February 15, 1972; or

        (iii)   lack of national eligibility;

    (D)   has at least one author or rightholder who was, at the time the work was created, a national or domiciliary of an eligible country, and if published, was first published in an eligible country and not published in the United States during the 30-day period following publication in such eligible country; and

    (E)   if the source country for the work is an eligible country solely by virtue of its adherence to the WIPO Performances and Phonograms Treaty, is a sound recording.

(7)   The term "rightholder" means the person—

    (A)   who, with respect to a sound recording, first fixes a sound recording with authorization, or

    (B)   who has acquired rights from the person described in subparagraph (A) by means of any conveyance or by operation of law.

(8)   The "source country" of a restored work is—

    (A)   a nation other than the United States;

    (B)   in the case of an unpublished work—

        (i)   the eligible country in which the author or rightholder is a national or domiciliary, or, if a restored work has more than 1 author or rightholder, of which the majority of foreign authors or rightholders are nationals or domiciliaries; or

        (ii)   if the majority of authors or rightholders are not foreign, the nation other than the United States which has the most significant contacts with the work; and

    (C)   in the case of a published work—

        (i)   the eligible country in which the work is first published, or

        (ii)   if the restored work is published on the same day in 2 or more eligible countries, the eligible country which has the most significant contacts with the work.

DISCUSSION OF THE LAW

Although there is no one source of "international copyright law," because such laws are national in origin and differ from country to country, the United States has signed treaties, such as the Berne Convention for the Protection of Literary and Artistic Works, which provide that the United States will respect copyright laws from other signatory countries. The Berne Convention has been further expanded and adopted in the Agreement on Trade-Related Aspects of Intellectual Property Rights or the TRIPS agreement, to which the United States is also a signatory. Section 104 of the Copyright Act acknowledges these treaties and notes that at least for unpublished works, the United States will protect the copyright regardless of the nationality of the author.

There are very few countries that are not subject to the Berne Convention at this time. It is safer to assume that a country is a signatory to the Berne Convention than to assume the opposite. One of the very few countries that is not a signatory as of this writing is Iran, for instance. Even if a book is written by an Iranian author, however, it is protected by United States copyright if it is coauthored by a national or domiciliary of the United States or if it is first published in the United States or in a foreign nation that is a Berne Convention member state. Even if the work by the Iranian author is first published in Iran, it is still protected by copyright in the United States if it is published in the United States or a treaty party within thirty days after first publication in Iran. As you can see, then, most foreign published works will be protected by copyright laws of the United States.

For works published before the United States entered into the Berne Convention and still retained formality requirements for copyright protection (such as the requirement to include a copyright notice on the work), the Copyright Act restores the copyright in foreign works that otherwise fail to comply with the requirements of United States law. The work is generally restored unless it would have entered the public domain in its native country prior to January 1, 1996.[1]

COMMON SCENARIOS

⊃ **A faculty member has located a rare collection of German books published in the 1930s with a copyright notice. The faculty member**

wishes to digitize the books and make them publicly viewable (not downloadable) through the library's website. Can the books be digitized and made available?

These books would be subject to copyright restoration under the Uruguay Round Agreement Act. So, even if a work does not contain a copyright notice or the registration was not properly renewed with the United States Copyright Office, the work would remain protected for the entire term of the copyright if it has not entered the public domain in the United States. One exception to this rule would be if the work had entered the public domain in its native country (in this case, Germany) prior to January 1, 1996. Works from the 1930s in Germany would not have entered the public domain in Germany before 1996; therefore, the copyright in the United States would extend for ninety-five years from the date of publication, or until around 2025. However, note that works within the last twenty years of copyright protection can be reproduced, digitized, and displayed by libraries in the United States pursuant to Section 108(h) so long as the work is not subject to normal commercial exploitation, the work cannot be obtained at a reasonable price, and no notice has been filed with the U.S. Copyright Office to that effect. Section 108(h) does not specify whether it applies to international works.[2] As such, one could interpret Section 108(h) to permit both domestic and foreign works within the last twenty years of the copyright term to permit digitization. In this case, the works were not available commercially, nor were they being sold on the commercial market (and the United States Copyright Office has received none of the aforementioned notices to date). Thus, the librarian could conclude that the German works could be digitized as part of the library's digital collection.

⊃ A librarian from an academic library wishes to digitize and display a copy of a book from Iran published in 1990. Can they digitize and publicly display the book?

Iran is one of the few countries that is not a party to the Berne Convention. Thus, generally speaking, other countries are not bound to respect the copyright laws of Iran. However, as noted in the discussion above, it would still be protected by United States copyright law if it was coauthored by a national or domiciliary of the United States or if it had first been published in the United States. Thus, the answer may be yes, but a little bit more research as to the nationality and domestic status of the author as well as the location of the first publication of the book may be necessary first.

TOOLS & RESOURCES

Enriquez, Ana. "International & Foreign Copyright: An American Perspective." Presentation, DPLAfest, Chicago, 2019. https://static.sched.com/hosted _files/dplafest2019/b6/20190416%20International%20and%20 Foreign%20Copyright%20for%20DPLAFest.pptx. CC BY.

The Scholarly Communications Outreach librarian from Pennsylvania State University, Ana Enriquez, has created a wonderful interactive workshop about international copyright for DPLAfest 2019. The presentation materials are available under a CC BY license.

U.S. Copyright Office. *International Copyright Relations of the United States.* Circular 38A, revised 2021. https://www.copyright.gov/circs/circ38a.pdf.

This guide explains international issues and copyright.

U.S. Copyright Office. *Copyright Restoration under the URAA.* Circular 38B, revised 2013. https://www.copyright.gov/circs/circ38b.pdf.

This guide explains the restoration of foreign copyrights.

World Intellectual Property Organization. "Berne Convention for the Protection of Literary and Artistic Works." https://www.wipo.int/treaties/en/ip/berne/.

The text of the Berne Convention.

NOTES

1. But note that there is some conflict here, at least in the Ninth Circuit Court of Appeals, which has ruled that a foreign work published abroad before 1925 with no copyright notice and never published in the United States is still not in the public domain in the United States (citing *Twin Books Corp. v. Walt Disney Co.*, 83 F.3d 1162 (9th Cir. 1996)). Also note, however, that Nimmer, a premier treatise on copyright law, disagrees emphatically with this court ruling. 3 Nimmer on Copyright § 9.12 (2020)

2. If the work had been published in Germany without a copyright notice, it would be unclear how the Ninth Circuit *Twin Books* decision would impact this analysis. As Nimmer notes: "Even a very old work never published in the U.S. (and never published abroad with a copyright notice) could potentially qualify" for continued protection in the United States. 3 Nimmer on Copyright § 9.12 (2020) (citing *Twin Books Corp. v. Walt Disney Co.*, 83 F.3d 1162 (9th Cir. 1996)).

CHAPTER 14

The Implied
License Doctrine

Title 17, Section 204: Execution of Transfers of Copyright Ownership

(a)   A transfer of copyright ownership, other than by operation of law, is not valid unless an instrument of conveyance, or a note or memorandum of the transfer, is in writing and signed by the owner of the rights conveyed or such owner's duly authorized agent.

DISCUSSION OF THE LAW

While an exclusive transfer of copyright must be made in writing as noted in Section 204 of the Copyright Act, nonexclusive transfers of copyright may "be granted orally, or may even be implied from conduct . . . when the totality of the parties' conduct indicates an intent to grant such permission."[1] This doctrine stems from contract law; therefore, as with any contract, the specifics of the contractual terms "should be reasonably clear."[2]

While some courts find that specific factors indicate the intent, through an implied license, to transfer nonexclusive rights, such as "when (1) a person (the licensee) requests the creation of a work, (2) the creator (the licensor) makes that particular work and delivers it to the licensee who requested it, and (3) the licensor intends that the licensee-requestor copy and distribute his work,"[3] what is most important is "whether the totality of the parties' conduct supports the existence of a non-exclusive license."[4]

Case Study: Dissertation Author Sues University

One particular case is worth mentioning in this discussion because it stemmed from an author of a dissertation suing a library for digitizing and cataloging the dissertation without the author's permission. In *Diversey v. Schmidly*, the plaintiff sued the University of New Mexico for unlawfully copying and distributing (through the library and by providing a copy to ProQuest) his unpublished dissertation.[5] The plaintiff was a PhD student who submitted a draft copy of his dissertation for review, and claimed the university copied and distributed the draft without his permission. The Court of Appeals for the Tenth Circuit rejected the "continuing wrong" minority test for tolling the statute of limitations and held that the student was barred from claiming damages for the unlawful reproduction of his dissertation because he knew that they had made copies longer than three years before filing the lawsuit.[6] However, the plaintiff was only alerted that the work was distributed through the library and Proquest within three years of filing the lawsuit, so his claims were permitted to go forward.[7] Why include a discussion of this particular case in the "implied license" portion of this book when the case centered mainly around a discussion of tolling the statute of limitations for filing a copyright infringement lawsuit? Because one of the arguments made by the administrators in their defense was that they had an "implied license" to keep and distribute the work.[8] That particular claim was not even addressed at the appellate court level and, as such, seemed to have failed. The Appellate Court also found that the university's fair use defense did not protect it from potential liability for distributing the unpublished dissertation because "only the first factor—the purpose and character of use"—weighed in the university's favor.[9]

COMMON SCENARIOS

⊃ **Your library has a legacy collection of theses and dissertations from the 1950s. You do not have any written license from the authors of the works. The institutional repository manager has approached you to ask whether it is permissible, under a theory of implied license, to digitize the collection. Is it?**
Of course, the copyright owner of the thesis/dissertation is the author. Today, many institutional repositories obtain a nonexclusive license from the author to preserve and distribute theses and dissertations. However, the likelihood that the library can locate and obtain any such written documents from the 1950s is slim. Putting aside issues related to alumni relations, which may prevent some libraries from digitizing these collections out of a worry of upsetting unsuspecting alumni, can the university argue that it has an implied

license to these works? Using the three-part test laid out above, the first two factors do seem to be met: the university requested that the author create the work to fulfill an academic requirement, and the author delivered the work to the university. The third factor seems more questionable: did the author intend for the university to copy and distribute the work? Probably not. As copyright expert Kevin Smith points out, if the university only distributes the copy that was deposited, there might be a first sale argument; but as soon as the library makes copies of the dissertation, other issues arise.[10] In a case under very similar circumstances, discussed above, an author sued his university for infringement and was permitted to pursue damages. (In that case, the court notes that the defendant university officials "believed they had 'certain non-exclusive rights in the dissertation, e.g., an implied license to keep copies of the dissertation at the University Libraries and to catalog the work.'"[11]) So, likely it would be best to proceed with caution in these instances and avoid mass digitization or distribution of old but in-copyright dissertations and theses. Note that the date of the work in this scenario is the 1950s and not a much-older work, which may be in the public domain (depending on whether the work is considered "published" or not).

⊃ **A professor wishes to enter student work into the institutional repository, so the syllabus includes a statement that reads: "The final project for this course will be entered into the institutional repository and made available to the general public." Is there an implied license from the students in the course to put their final project into the institutional repository (IR)?**

The short answer is yes. This example was detailed in a blog post for Duke Library by Smith, where he points out that the three factors for an implied license are present here: "There is an offer made—in exchange for a grade and credit in this course, you will give the school a license for IR deposit. And when the work is handed in, there is a performance from which acceptance of that offer is readily implied."[12] He does note—and I agree—that whether the professor (and the library) *can* do this is different from whether they *should* do it. It would likely be much more palatable to the students to give them a choice as to whether they wish to have their work preserved in the institutional repository and, in that instance, to have them self-deposit the work and sign a nonexclusive license in the process. There also may be additional privacy and Family Educational Rights and Privacy Act (FERPA) issues to be aware of, as well, which reach beyond the scope of this book.

TOOLS & RESOURCES

Enriquez, Ana. "Licensing Track Workshop: Understanding the Implied License Doctrine." Presentation, Kraemer Copyright Conference, University of Colorado, Colorado Springs, June 11, 2019. Available at https://copyright.uccs.edu/2019/session/licensing-track-workshop. CC BY 4.0.

This conference presentation by Ana Enriquez, the Scholarly Communications Outreach librarian at Penn State University Libraries, succinctly lays out the basics of the implied license doctrine.

Lipton, Jacqui. "Implied Licenses in Copyright Law." Authors Alliance, May 27, 2020. https://www.authorsalliance.org/2020/05/27/implied-licenses-in-copyright-law/.

Jacqui Lipton explains the implied license doctrine in a guest post for the Authors Alliance website.

NOTES

1. Nimmer on Copyright § 10.03 (2020).
2. *Id.*
3. *Id.* (citing cases from a variety of jurisdictions including the Seventh Circuit Court of Appeals).
4. *Id.* (citing *Baisden v. I'm Ready Prods., Inc.*, 693 F.3d 491, 501 (5th Cir. 2012)).
5. See 738 F.3d 1196 (10th Cir. 2013).
6. *Id.* at 1202.
7. *Id.* at 1203.
8. *Id.* at 1199n1.
9. *Id.* at 1203.
10. Kevin Smith, "Copyright Roundup," *Scholarly Communications @ Duke*, December 27, 2013, https://blogs.library.duke.edu/scholcomm/2013/12/27/copyright-roundup/.
11. *Diversey v. Schmidly*, 738 F.3d 1196, 1199 n.1 (10th Cir. 2013).
12. Kevin Smith, "The Truth about Contracts," *Scholarly Communications @ Duke*, February 13, 2015, https://blogs.library.duke.edu/scholcomm/2015/02/13/truth-contracts/.

CHAPTER 15

Sovereign Immunity

United States Constitution, Eleventh Amendment
The judicial power of the United States shall not be construed to extend to any suit in law or equity, commenced or prosecuted against one of the United States by citizens of another state, or by citizens or subjects of any foreign state.

DISCUSSION OF THE LAW

Although the Eleventh Amendment does not specifically prevent citizens of a particular state from suing their own government for damages, it has long been interpreted by courts to do just that.[1] Under the Eleventh Amendment, then, state governments and governmental actors, such as public universities, cannot be sued for copyright damages. However, Congress attempted to abrogate state sovereign immunity to copyright lawsuits in the Copyright Remedy Clarification Act (CRCA) of 1990.[2] However, the United States Supreme Court, in *Allen v. Cooper*, ruled that the act failed to abrogate sovereign immunity because Congress, in passing the act, did not appropriately link the "scope of its abrogation to the redress or prevention of unconstitutional injuries."[3] Therefore, currently states still have sovereign immunity from copyright damages; however, Congress could still attempt to pass another law abrogating state sovereign immunity for copyright damages should they find sufficient evidence of unconstitutional injuries. After the decision in *Allen v. Cooper* was released, Senator Thom Tillis of North Carolina asked the United States Copyright Office to conduct a sovereign immunity study assessing the damages, if any, caused by a lack of copyright liability to plaintiffs from state actors. In response, the United States Copyright Office called for public comments responding to a sovereign immunity study and held a public roundtable asking for public response.[4] I participated in both, and you will find links to the documents in the "Tools & Resources" section below. The results of this study remain to be seen; generally speaking, I found the "evidence" that sovereign immunity abrogation is necessary due to constitutional harms to be wholly lacking, as I discussed in my podcast (see also below).

Note that even though public universities can avail themselves of sovereign immunity to avoid damages from copyright infringement lawsuits, that does not mean public institutions should avoid copyright law or use sovereign immunity as a sword instead of a limited shield. It is important to note, of course, that a plaintiff may still be able to sue government actors, asking for an injunction, rather than damages, relating from copyright infringement under the *Ex parte Young* doctrine.

Case Study: Georgia State University

The Georgia State University electronic reserves lawsuit was mentioned above, in chapter 10, "Fair Use." Here, there is a different reason to discuss the twelve-year lawsuit. As discussed above, Georgia State University ultimately prevailed on eighty-nine of the claims and was successful in defending the lawsuit stemming from its electronic reserves system. However, no university would wish to go through a similar lawsuit. Georgia State University did avail itself of sovereign immunity and, as such, could not be sued for damages. However, the lawsuit for injunctive relief under the *Ex parte Young* doctrine lasted for twelve years before it was finally concluded, and Georgia State was not awarded attorney's fees and had to bear the costs of the litigation.[5] Again, although the outcome was overall in favor of Georgia State University, defending a lawsuit for twelve years is no small endeavor.

COMMON SCENARIOS

⊃ **A public university professor posted a copyrighted picture to their personal web page and received a notice of infringement. The professor contacts general counsel of the university for advice. Does sovereign immunity apply?**

No. If the professor used a personal website that was not created for university purposes, the sovereign immunity provision would not protect them from potential copyright damages. They may have a viable fair use defense depending on the circumstances, but they would not be able to assert sovereign immunity.

⊃ **A public university receives a copyright infringement claim due to a photograph posted on a university website. Can the university assert sovereign immunity as a defense?**

Yes—however, it is best for the university to proceed first by reaching out to the author and offering to remove the offending photograph before immediately asserting sovereign immunity. There may be other defenses, such as fair use, that may apply as well, and it is a good idea to try to work with the rights owner to avoid litigation in the first place (potentially by paying a licensing fee and removing the photograph), rather than fighting out the case in court.

⊃ **A public university is sued for posting copies of books and other copyrighted materials on electronic reserves. Can the university assert sovereign immunity as a defense?**

Yes, and in fact, in the case on which this hypothetical is based, *Cambridge University Press v. Becker*, Georgia State University did assert sovereign immunity.[6] Unfortunately, the university could still be sued for an injunction, and in that particular case the lawsuit lasted twelve years. So, sovereign immunity does not prevent costly, lengthy lawsuits; but it will prevent the university from being held liable for large damages, rather than receiving an injunction. (Note that the university still had to pay for its own attorney's fees in the *Cambridge University Press* case, which were not small).

TOOLS & RESOURCES

Benson, Sara, and Douglas Shontz. "Our Take on the Copyright Office Sovereign Immunity Roundtables." *Copyright Chat Podcast,* December 23, 2020. Available at https://www.library.illinois.edu/scp/podcast/our-take-on-the-copyright-office-sovereign-immunity-roundtables/.

My and Douglas Shontz's views on the Copyright Office's Sovereign Immunity Roundtable Discussions, as discussed on the *Copyright Chat Podcast*. Available through the University of Illinois's Scholarly Communication and Publishing Unit.

U.S. Copyright Office. State Sovereign Immunity Study. 2020. https://www.copyright.gov/policy/state-sovereign-immunity/.

The U.S. Copyright Office conducted this study with public comments and a public roundtable discussion session; the roundtable transcript is part of the coverage available online.

NOTES

1. See *Allen v. Cooper*, 140 S.Ct. 994, 1000 (2020).
2. *Id.* at 999.
3. *Id.* at 1007.
4. U.S. Copyright Office, "State Sovereign Immunity Study," https://www.copyright.gov/policy/state-sovereign-immunity/.
5. *Cambridge Univ. Press v. Becker*, Slip Op., No. 08 Civ. 1425 (N.D. Georgia Sept. 29, 2020).
6. *Id.*

CHAPTER 16

Copyright Metadata and Rights Statements

Note: this chapter provides no summary of "the law" because there are no laws governing metadata for copyright. However, the Digital Public Library of America (DPLA) and Europeana, the web portal of the European Union, did create a system for providing metadata for copyright called standardized rights statements. That system is summarized below. The section titled "Standardized Rights Statements" was originally part of a chapter written by Sara R. Benson: "Copyright Conundrums: Rights Issues in the Digitization of Library Collections" in *Digital Preservation in Libraries: Preparing for a Sustainable Future*, edited by Jeremy Myntti and Jessalyn Zoom (Chicago: American Library Association, 2019). © 2019 American Library Association.

DISCUSSION OF THE LAW

Standardized Rights Statements

The standardized rights statements were launched in April 2016 by the DPLA and Europeana to create an unambiguous, uniform system for inputting rights metadata.[1] There are three main categories of rights statements contained in the standardized rights statements:

- In Copyright
- No Copyright
- Other

The three categories are further subdivided into more specific categories. For "In Copyright" works, for instance, the additional subcategories include the following:

- In Copyright
- In Copyright—Educational Use Permitted
- In Copyright—Non-Commercial Use Permitted
- In Copyright—Rightsholder(s) Unlocatable or Unidentifiable

The simplest subcategory for "In Copyright" is just that—"In Copyright."[2] When a work is clearly still protected by copyright and the rightsholder is known, this statement is appropriate. The next two designations listed above permit noncommercial or educational uses only.[3] Finally, a designation for "Unlocatable or Unidentifiable Rights Holder" is appropriate when the work is clearly still in the copyright term, but the rightsholder is unknown—this would be appropriate for an orphan work.[4] Each category of rights statements is fully described and detailed both on the SRS website and in the SRS White Paper (http://rightsstatements.org/en/; http://rightsstatements.org/files/180531recom mendations_for_standardized_international_rights_statements_v1.2.2.pdf).

The "No Copyright" rights statements further subdivide into four categories:

- No Copyright—Contractual Restrictions
- No Copyright—Non-Commercial Use Only
- No Copyright—Other Known Legal Restrictions
- No Copyright—United States[5]

The first category, "No Copyright—Contractual Restrictions," would be appropriate if a work is no longer under the copyright term restrictions, but by license or contractual obligation the work has additional restrictions.[6] So, for instance, if a vendor has commercialized a public domain work and has imposed terms of use, this designation would be appropriate. The "No Copyright— Non-Commercial Use Only" designation would be appropriate for works that are designated with a license to be open, but only for noncommercial uses.[7] The "No Copyright—Other Known Legal Restrictions" designation would be appropriate if the work is not restricted by copyright, but rather by other legal rights, such as privacy or moral rights.[8] Finally, the "No Copyright—United States" designation would be an appropriate license for U.S. public domain materials, such as those published in the United States prior to 1925.[9] This standardized rights statement type is designated as "United States" because public domain terms can vary by country and by one country's treatment of foreign works under its own law (such as the restoration of foreign copyrights under U.S. law), and this statement has only been vetted for the U.S. public domain term.[10]

The "Other" category is akin to providing catchall provisions. It is broken down into three subcategories:[11]

- Copyright Not Evaluated
- Copyright Undetermined
- No Known Copyright

"Copyright Not Evaluated" is a provision that lets the user know the copyright has yet to be evaluated by the hosting institution in any way—for instance, with the mass digitization of works. Although the digitizing institution may believe that the materials it is digitizing belong in the public domain, it has not done an individualized assessment of each piece in the collection. The "Copyright Undetermined" designation is intended for use when the institution has reviewed an item and has "made the item available, but the organization was unable to make a conclusive determination as to the copyright status of the item."[12] A library may wish to use this designation if, for instance, it has performed a copyright review, but was unable to determine the status of the item because the author's death date is unknown and it is necessary to calculate copyright length. Finally, "No Known Copyright" is an appropriate designation for a work made between 1925 and 1968 where a reasonably diligent online search has been conducted and no copyright can be located.[13] It indicates that this is not a simple case (like a work published in the United States prior to 1925 would be), and that a copyright search has been made, but that the organization cannot warrant the accuracy of the information to an infallible degree.

Note that all the rights statements include a disclaimer that there is no warranty as to the accuracy of the rights statement and that the user of the work is ultimately responsible for their own use.

Traditional Knowledge Labels

For countries that have protection for moral rights or a sui generis law protecting the right to traditional cultural expression, or for anyone wishing to recognize community rights that are not generally protected under U.S. copyright law, the Traditional Knowledge Labels (TK Labels) are available as "an educative and non-legal intervention."[14] The TK Labels were designed to address "the enormous amounts of indigenous cultural heritage material that circulates without indigenous perspectives or protocols regarding fair and equitable circulation and use."[15] There are currently eighteen labels available, inspired by the Creative

Commons licensing schema to specify how to appropriately engage with indigenous cultural heritage material. A deeper description of the appropriate use of TK Labels is available both on the Local Contexts website and in a detailed article written by Kimberly Christen.[16]

Case Study: Slavish Reproductions

There are a few copyright cases involving instances where someone intended to create an exact replica of an object or photo and wished to claim a new copyright in the replication. In one case, a photographer took a picture of paintings that were in the public domain.[17] The photographer then claimed to own a copyright in the photograph. The court held that the photograph was just a "slavish replication" of the photo and, as such, no new copyright attached to it because there was no originality.[18] A similar scenario exists with library digitization processes: the library digitizing a collection does not own a copyright in the slavish copy it has made of another work. Similarly, when a firm created digital models of a car designed by Toyota, the court found that the model was nothing more than a slavish reproduction of the car design, and thus the firm had no independent copyright.[19]

COMMON SCENARIOS

⊃ **Your library has a collection of unpublished photographs taken by a single American photographer in the 1930s that it wishes to digitize and share with the public. Can the library put a Creative Commons license on the collection?**
Generally, no. Usually libraries collect materials but do not own the copyright for the materials. See the case study above noting that the slavish reproduction itself does not create an independent copyright. The rare exception to this rule is when the author (in this case, the photographer) has transferred copyright to the library in writing or if employees of the library took the photographs in the scope of their employment (noting, of course, that many faculty own their own copyrights). Thus, what the library really needs to do in this case—assuming the library does not own the copyright in the collection—is to determine the copyright status of the works in the collection and apply appropriate rights statements to the collection to alert the public as to the copyright status of the works in the collection. This may not be simple, especially if the photographs were

taken by multiple photographers and if some photographs were published while others were unpublished.

If the collection is by a single author, however, and all the photographs were unpublished, then a single rights statement may be applicable to all the photographs in the collection. (Note that there may be other legal issues to take into account prior to making a decision to digitize the collection, such as privacy rights, contractual limitations, ethical concerns, and the like).

In this case, the photographer died before 1950, therefore the works are in the public domain in the United States and can be digitized. The library can put a "No Copyright—United States" rights statement on the collection, which will alert the public that the works are in the public domain in the United States.

⊃ **A library has a collection of newspaper articles from the 1950s that it wishes to digitize. It would like to put a public domain rights statement on the collection. Can the library appropriately put a public domain statement on the entire collection?**

In the case of newspapers, there are likely multiple copyright owners involved in the collection. While the newspaper owns the copyright to most of the content, there may be some photographs, advertisements, and other insert types, such as cartoons that are not owned by the newspaper publisher. Thus, even if the newspaper's copyright was not properly renewed and the paper is in the public domain, there are portions that may not be in the public domain. It may still be entirely appropriate for the library to digitize and distribute the newspapers (along with all the content) under fair use, but which rights statement should be applied to the collection? In this case, the library may wish to use the "In Copyright—Educational Use Permitted" and to explain further that the main text of the newspaper is in the public domain, but the inserts, such as advertisements and cartoons, may still be in copyright.

⊃ **A library is in the process of digitizing photographs that were taken recently of public domain artwork and sculptures. The photographs in the collection were taken by many different artists. The library would like to put a public domain license on the collection. Can the library do so?**

Generally speaking, yes. Courts have held that when a public work is reproduced in a "slavish production," meaning adding nothing to it, no copyright is added to the work. Thus, the original artwork and sculptures are in the public domain, and so are the photographs of those works, assuming they were taken to simply replicate the works (and add nothing original or new).

TOOLS & RESOURCES

Benson, Sara R., and Hannah Stitzlein. "Copyright and Digital Collections: A Data-Driven Roadmap for Rights Statement Success." *College & Research Libraries* 81, no. 5 (2020): 753. https://crl.acrl.org/index.php/crl/article/view/24510.

This open-access research article provides a road map for cultural heritage organizations applying rights statements to their digital collections.

Digital Public Library of America. "Rights Statements 101 Webinar." https://medium.com/open-glam/dpla-presents-rights-statements-101-webinar-a84dcc590a4e.

This webinar explains how to use rights statements.

Digital Public Library of America. The Rights Portal. https://rights-portal.dp.la/.

In their words: "Rights resources for American cultural heritage organizations." A website compiling useful tools and examples to those using the DPLA rights statements for their digital collections.

RightsStatements.org. https://rightsstatements.org/en/.

The rights statements and explanations for how to implement them are available at this consortium website.

Sims, Nancy. "Rights, Ethics, Accuracy, and Open Licenses in Online Collections: What's 'Ours' Isn't Really Ours." *College & Research Libraries News* 78, no. 2 (2017): 79–82. https://crln.acrl.org/index.php/crlnews/article/view/9620/11028.

This open-access article explains why libraries cannot claim copyright for many of their digitized collections.

NOTES

1. The Digital Public Library of America (https://dp.la/info/) is an online collection of cultural heritage materials from American museums and libraries. Europeana (www.europeana.eu) is a digital collection of cultural heritage materials from European museums and libraries.

See also International Rights Statements Working Group, "White Paper: Recommendations for Standardized International Rights Statements" (October 2015, last updated May 2018), https://rightsstatements.org/files/180531recommendations_for_standardized_international _rights_statements_v1.2.2.pdf.

2. International Rights Statements Working Group, "White Paper," 20.
3. *Id.* at 24–25.
4. *Id.* at 23.
5. *Id.* at 26–30.
6. *Id.* at 27.
7. *Id.* at 26.
8. *Id.* at 28. In the United States, the only recognized "moral rights" are those contained in the Visual Artists Rights Act (VARA): 17 U.S.C. § 106A (2012). In other countries, however, moral rights may include rights such as attribution and integrity (including rights against the mutilation of the work) and may last indefinitely. Cyrill Rigamonti, "Deconstructing Moral Rights," *Harvard International Law Journal* 47, no. 2 (2006): 357.
9. International Rights Statements Working Group, *supra*, at 29.
10. *Id.*
11. *Id.* at 30–31.
12. *Id.* at 31.
13. rightsstatements.org, "Copyright Undetermined," http://rightsstatements.org/vocab/ UND/1.0/.
14. Local Contexts, "TK Licenses," https://localcontexts.org/licenses/traditional-knowledge -licenses/.
15. *Id.*
16. Kimberly Christen, "Tribal Archives, Traditional Knowledge, and Local Contexts: Why the 's' Matters," *Journal of Western Archives* 6, no. 1 (2015): 1–19.
17. *Bridgeman Art Library, Ltd. v. Corel Corp.*, 36 F. Supp. 2d 191 (S.D.N.Y. 1999).
18. *Id.* at 197.
19. *Meshwerks v. Toyota*, 528 F.3d 1258, 1270 (10th Cir. 2008).

CHAPTER 17

Controlled Digital Lending

Note: this chapter provides no summary of "the law" because there are no specific laws directly addressing controlled digital lending; rather, it is a legal theory that stems from the right of first sale and the fair use doctrine. However, the legal analysis providing a basis for this type of library lending is summed up in a white paper by David R. Hansen and Kyle K. Courtney; see "Tools & Resources," below.

DISCUSSION OF THE LAW

Controlled digital lending is a practice of library lending that stems from a few different sources of library-lending rights, including the right of first sale and fair use. The courts have addressed in limited circumstances whether there can be a digital right of first sale and concluded (so far) that there is not.[1] However, when the right of first sale is combined with a right to fair use, the argument in favor of controlled digital lending becomes stronger—especially for works no longer subject to commercial exploitation.[2] Under this practice, the HathiTrust Digital Library has been lending in-copyright books for one-hour renewable periods (for viewing only) to member libraries on a one-to-one basis, thanks to the Emergency Temporary Access Service (ETAS). In other words, if the library has submitted a book into the HathiTrust corpus by digitizing an in-copyright book, a verified member of that library can check out a view-only version of that book for an hour at a time.[3] If the library has multiple physical copies of the book in its collection, then patrons can check out as many copies of the digital version as the library has physical copies of the book. This practice has been made possible during the COVID-19 pandemic because libraries are less able to lend the physical book copies and is justified under emergency fair use principles. Note that the Internet Archive has been lending materials under an analysis of controlled digital lending as well, but without some of the safeguards provided by the HathiTrust ETAS terms, and has been sued for their practice.[4]

Case Study: Orphan Works and Controlled Digital Lending

An orphan work is an out-of-print work for which the copyright owner is unknown. This status could be due to many factors, including multiple transfers of the copyright, a copyright owner (publisher) going out of business, or unclear heirs of a deceased author. When a work is an orphan, it is often not commercially available on the marketplace for obvious reasons—if the work were still being distributed, the copyright owner would be clear. This does not mean, of course, that such works are less important. An orphan work could be critical to researchers and students. So, what is to be done when the copyright owner is unknown but a work is requested nonetheless? Of course, the work could be viewed in person, or the physical work could be lent out; but if a work is no longer being reproduced and sold, a library might be loath to exercise its first sale rights by lending the physical work because if the copy is lost there may be no way to replace it.

Fair use can be of assistance here. In fact, the University of Michigan was preparing to engage in a digitization project whereby orphan works would be digitized and available on the basis of controlled digital lending.[5] Unfortunately, the Orphan Works Project (OWP) was put on hold because "the screening process was not adequately distinguishing between orphan works (which were to be included in the OWP) and in-print works (which were not)."[6] To date, the OWP has not been reinstated. See also the *Orphan Works and Mass Digitization Report*, in "Tools & Resources."

COMMON SCENARIOS

⊃ **Your library is a member of the HathiTrust Digital Library and wishes to participate in the HathiTrust Emergency Temporary Access Service. Is this a good idea?**

The first thing to keep in mind is that this service is not always available. It was created during the 2020/21 COVID-19 pandemic due to extenuating circumstances. Thus, it was available to libraries that were not open to their patrons. If your library is fully open, this service would not be appropriate. That said, each library needs to do their own risk assessment to decide whether to participate.

The ETAS takes advantage of fair use, but fair use is not without risk. Once the library has the support of general counsel, it can proceed with the ETAS.

⟳ **Your library has a collection of orphan works. It wishes to make them available to library patrons through controlled digital lending. Should the library make these works available digitally through controlled digital lending?**

This very much depends on how comfortable your library is with assuming some level of legal risk. If a work is no longer being published and is unlikely to have any kind of market value, the fair use argument is strong. However, if a copyright owner finds out that their work is being digitally lent out (even on a one-to-one basis, comparing to the number of physical copies held by the library), they could choose to sue. This is actually one of the projects the University of Michigan Library was engaging in when it was sued originally for its use of the search function in the HathiTrust case. When the lawsuit began, the Orphan Works Project was put on hold and as of this writing has not resumed (see the case study above for more information).

TOOLS & RESOURCES

Hansen, David R., and Kyle K. Courtney. "A White Paper on Controlled Digital Lending of Library Books." Controlled Digital Lending by Libraries, 2018. https://controlleddigitallending.org/whitepaper.

This white paper provides the basis for library controlled digital lending grounded in the right of first sale and fair use.

HathiTrust Digital Library. "HathiTrust Emergency Temporary Access Service: Terms of Service." Updated January 12, 2021. https://www.hathitrust.org/etas-terms-of-service.

The HathiTrust website explains the ETAS and provides the terms of service explaining that the lending library can lend only as many copies of a digital work as it has in its physical collection.

U.S. Copyright Office. Orphan Works and Mass Digitization: A Report of the Register of Copyrights (2015). https://www.copyright.gov/orphan/reports/orphan-works2015.pdf.

If you are interested in orphan works, you can find detailed analyses of copyright issues involving orphan works in this resource.

NOTES

1. *Capitol Records, LLC v. Redigi Inc.*, 910 F.3d 649 (2d Cir. 2018).
2. David R. Hansen and Kyle K. Courtney, "A White Paper on Controlled Digital Lending of Library Books" (Controlled Digital Lending by Libraries, 2018), https://controlleddigitallending.org/whitepaper. CC BY 4.0.
3. HathiTrust Digital Library, "Emergency Temporary Access Service," https://www.hathitrust.org/ETAS-Description.
4. *Hachette Book Group, Inc. v. Internet Archive*, 20-CV-04160 (S.D.N.Y. June 1, 2020), available at https://www.eff.org/document/complaint-50.
5. *Authors Guild, Inc. v. HathiTrust*, 755 F.3d 87, 92 (2d Cir. 2014).
6. *Id.*

CHAPTER 18

Creative Commons Licensing

Note: this chapter provides no summary of "the law" because there are no specific laws directly addressing Creative Commons (CC) licensing. Rather the licenses are enforced under basic concepts of contract law.

DISCUSSION OF THE LAW

A license is a contract. Normally, a license occurs between a specified number of parties, such as a publisher and an author or multiple authors. However, in the case of CC licensing, the author designates a license to members of the general public. Only the copyright owner can put a CC license on a work. because it is the copyright owner's right to decide how the work should be used.

There are a variety of CC licenses to choose from, depending on how the copyright owner wishes to permit others to use the work without first asking for permission. There are a few things to note that are important and apply to all CC licenses. First, they are irrevocable, so the author or authors deciding to apply a license should do so after careful consideration. Second, CC licenses are always subject to fair use, so even if a given license would generally prohibit a certain use, if it is otherwise a fair use, it is permitted. Third, courts generally enforce a CC license under contract law principles, so it should be treated as a legally enforceable contract. Fourth, even if a particular use is not permitted under a CC license, you can always contact the copyright owner to ask whether they will grant you an individual nonexclusive license to engage in your intended activity. CC licenses simply allow the public to understand what may be done with copyrighted works without obtaining specific, individual permission, but they do not prevent you from reaching out to the copyright owner to ask for an individual license.

There is nothing incompatible with using both a copyright notice and a CC license. The copyright notice indicates who owns the copyright to the work, and the CC license lets the public know how the copyright owner intends for the public to use the work without first obtaining specific permission.

The license options under Creative Commons range from designating a work in the public domain with a CCo license to restricting uses to nonderivative uses only, using an ND designation. I have laid out the different kinds of licenses below, including a brief description of the license terms, beginning with the least restrictive license and moving into the most restrictive license. Of course, for all the licensing terms and for the most up-to-date terms, it is best to go directly to the Creative Commons website, https://creativecommons.org.

- CCo: designating a copyright protected work to the public domain
- CC BY: retaining copyright, but allowing any use of the work with proper attribution
- CC BY-SA: retaining copyright, but allowing any use of the work with proper attribution and requiring any derivative works created using the work to also include the same license—to "share alike"
- CC BY-NC: retaining copyright, but allowing any use of the work with proper attribution and requiring those using the work to do so only for noncommercial purposes
- CC BY-NC-SA: Retaining copyright, but allowing any use of the work with proper attribution and requiring those using the work to do so only for noncommercial purposes and requiring any derivative works created using the work to also include the same license, thus forbidding any commercial use of the work
- CCBY-ND: retaining copyright, but allowing use of the work with proper attribution as long as the new work does not change the original work or constitute a derivative work ("nonderivative")
- CCBY-NC-ND: retaining copyright, but allowing use of the work with proper attribution as long as the new work does not change the original work or constitute a derivative work and requiring those using the work to do so only for noncommercial purposes.

Figure 18.1 shows these licenses as a stack with the most open—public domain—at the top.

There are a few common areas of confusion surrounding CC licenses. One is the use of the "share alike" (SA) designation in a license. Many believe that if the SA designation is used on a particular work, all new works incorporating that

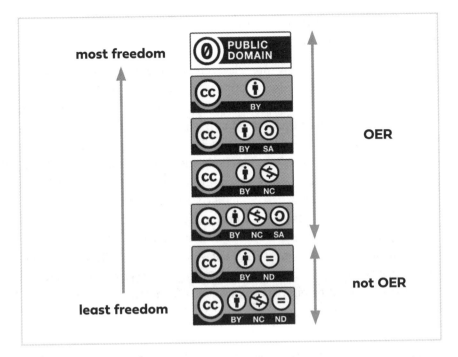

FIGURE 18.1 CC Licenses Chart

Source: Image adapted from Cable Green, "Updated Keynote Slides," 2014, https://www.slideshare.net/cgreen/updated-keynote-slides-october-2014. CC BY 4.0.

work must also use the same license. That is not true. Actually, the SA license only requires that new works that create a derivative using the work with the SA license must use that same license. (See the Common Scenarios section below for a specific explanation of this misconception.) The definition of what constitutes a derivative work is a legal one; see chapter 1, "Copyright Basics."

Another common area of confusion is what constitutes a "non-commercial" use under the NC license. Again, this is defined by the law, but the CC did a survey to determine how the public views "noncommercial" in the context of CC licenses. The CC conducted a study in 2008 on what internet users understand "noncommercial" to mean in the context of a CC license and concluded that "both creators and users generally consider uses that earn users money or involve online advertising to be commercial, while uses by organizations, by individuals, or for charitable purposes are less commercial but not decidedly noncommercial. Similarly, uses by for-profit companies are typically considered more commercial."[1] The CC has created a guide on non-commercial interpretation (see "Tools & Resources").

Case Study: Meaning of Noncommercial Creative Commons License

The Second Circuit Court of Appeals addressed the case of *Great Minds v. FedEx*. In that case, a school district printed out CC BY-NC-SA–licensed educational materials at FedEx.[2] The materials were created and copywritten by a nonprofit organization called Great Minds, who licensed the materials with a CC BY-NC-SA license. The court found that FedEx was merely acting as an agent of the school districts making justified copies under the noncommercial license. "Because FedEx acted as the mere agent of licensee school districts when it reproduced Great Minds' materials, and because there is no dispute that the school districts themselves sought to use Great Minds' materials for permissible purposes, we conclude that FedEx's activities did not breach the license or violate Great Minds' copyright."[3] Thus, unless a more specific licensing term is incorporated into the CC license, having a copying service provide the copies for a fee instead of printing out the copies yourself for a nonprofit or educational purpose does not violate the noncommercial CC license.

COMMON SCENARIOS

⊃ **The library has acquired a collection of books that are in the public domain. Can it put a CC0 license on them?**
Technically, only the owner of a copyright should put a Creative Commons license on a work. Here, using a rights statement would be more appropriate. It appears that the "No Copyright—United States" label would be appropriate here. For more information about rights statements, see chapter 16, "Copyright Metadata and Rights Statements."

⊃ **A library plans to host a public event to teach community members how to write poetry. The course uses a CC BY-NC–licensed booklet, and the planning committee wishes to charge a small fee to attendees to cover the cost of printing. Does this use violate the NC license?**
Probably not. Generally speaking, the noncommercial license is violated when groups intend to make a profit from using the work. Here, the library is simply charging for the cost of making the copies, not to make a profit, and the event is educational in nature.

⟳ **A library employee has created a guide to viewing a particular collection in the library along with descriptions (written by the employee) of the collection. The library employee wishes to put a Creative Commons license on the guide. Can they?**

It depends. Remember, only the copyright owner can put a Creative Commons license on a work. So, if the library employee owns the copyright to the guide, then the answer is yes. However, in many cases, the work would be considered owned by the library, not the employee, under the "work made for hire" doctrine (see chapter 1). If the employee works for an academic library and is a faculty member, then the employee likely owns the copyright. The key to understanding whether a Creative Commons license can be used, then, is understanding who owns the copyright to the guide.

TOOLS & RESOURCES

Creative Commons. https://creativecommons.org.

> The CC website includes many types of resources such as information about the different types of licenses, ways to search for materials that have been CC licensed, a CC license selector guide, and more.

Creative Commons. Certificate Resources. https://certificates.creativecommons .org/about/certificate-resources-cc-by/.

> Members of the public can learn about CC licenses through this certificate program. All the materials in the learning program are licensed with a CC BY 4.0 license.

Creative Commons. NonCommercial Interpretation. https://wiki.creative commons.org/wiki/NonCommercial_interpretation.

> Explains the meaning of the term "non-commercial" in the context of the CC licensing scheme.

NOTES

1. Creative Commons, Defining Noncommercial," April 26, 2014, https://wiki.creativecommons .org/wiki/Defining_Noncommercial. CC BY 4.0.
2. See *Great Minds v. FedEx Office & Print Servs., Inc.*, 886 F.3d 91 (2d Cir. 2018).
3. *Id.* at 92.

Fair Use Checklist

Name: _____ Date: _____ Project: _____

Institution: _____ Prepared by: _____

Purpose

Favoring Fair Use

❏ Teaching (including multiple copies for classroom use)
❏ Research
❏ Scholarship
❏ Nonprofit educational institution
❏ Criticism
❏ Comment
❏ News reporting
❏ Transformative use (alters the original work in a creative manner)
❏ Transformative use (uses the work for a purpose other than the original purpose)
❏ Restricted access (for only students or other appropriate group)
❏ Parody

Opposing Fair Use

❏ Commercial activity
❏ Profiting from the use
❏ Straight reproduction (copying without modification)
❏ Nontransformative use
❏ Entertainment
❏ Bad-faith behavior
❏ Denying credit to original author

Nature

Favoring Fair Use

❑ Published work

❑ Factual or nonfiction based

❑ Important to favored educational objectives

Opposing Fair Use

❑ Unpublished work

❑ Highly creative work (art, music, novels, films, plays)

❑ Fiction

❑ Consumable work (e.g., worksheets and standard exam forms)

Amount

Favoring Fair Use

❑ Small quantity

❑ Portion used is not central or significant to entire work

❑ Amount is tailored to meet the educational or other favored purpose

Opposing Fair Use

❑ Large portion or whole work used beyond the favored purpose

❑ Portion used could interfere with a reasonable market for the use (e.g., multiple chapters from a single book)

❑ Portion used is central to work or "heart of the work"

Effect

Favoring Fair Use

❑ User owns lawfully acquired or purchased copy of original work

❑ Few or modest number of copies made

❑ No significant effect on the market or potential market for copyrighted work

❑ No similar product marketed by the copyright holder

❑ Lack of a reasonable licensing mechanism for the work and the intended use

Opposing Fair Use

❑ Straight copying that is not transformative

❑ Portion used could interfere with a reasonable market for the use or derivatives (e.g., multiple chapters from a single book)

❑ Reasonably available licensing mechanism for the use of the copyrighted work

❑ Affordable permission available for using work

❑ Numerous copies made

❑ Posted to the Internet or otherwise made widely accessible

❑ Repeated or long-term use

Copyright and Film Screening Best Practices

This document is intended to help members of the university community determine when they must obtain a public performance license for a campus film screening or when a film screening may fall under one of the educational exemptions included in U.S. Copyright Law (17 U.S.C.).[1]

Screenings Requiring a Public Performance License

A public performance license is required when:

- the screening is being made purely for entertainment purposes—for instance, a "family night" screening of the movie *Frozen*, or the screening of the film *Premium Rush* in celebration of Bike Month
- the screening will be open to the entire campus, their family and friends, and/or members of the general public, even if the screening is being made for educational purposes
- the screening is part of a film festival that will be open to the entire campus, their family and friends, and/or members of the general public

If your screening requires a public performance license, please contact library media services for assistance in obtaining the license.

Screenings Not Requiring a Public Performance License

A screening arranged by a university academic department and/or a student club registered with the Office of Student Activities may not need public performance license if it falls within the parameters of the educational copyright exemptions found in sections 110(1) and 107 of U.S. Copyright Law.

Adapted from "Copyright & Film Screening Best Practices" by Carla Myers, assistant librarian and coordinator of Scholarly Communication, Miami University Libraries. CC BY 4.0.

For a campus film screening to qualify under these exemptions, it must be:

- sponsored by a student club registered with the Office of Student Activities and/or an academic department
- made for scholarly purposes in conjunction with the educational objectives of the student club and/or academic department, and include scholarly discussions or activities regarding the film as part of the screening
- limited to only those student and faculty members of the student group or those affiliated with the academic department
- lawfully obtained, which could include using a copy purchased by the university, the student group, or the department, or a copy obtained through the library. If the group sponsoring the showing needs assistance obtaining a lawfully acquired copy of a film, they should contact library media services. Under no circumstances should a film that has not been lawfully obtained (e.g., a bootlegged copy from the internet or a homemade copy of a commercial film) be used.

NOTE

1. 17 U.S.C. § 101 states that the public performance of an audiovisual work occurs when a film is performed or displayed "at a place open to the public or at any place where a substantial number of persons outside of a normal circle of a family and its social acquaintances is gathered."

APPENDIX C

Additional Recommended Reading and Materials

- American Library Association. CopyTalk Webinar Archive. http://www.ala .org/advocacy/copyright/copytalk.
- Benson, Sara R., host. *Copyright Chat Podcast.* https://www.library.illinois .edu/scp/copyright-overview/chat-podcast/.
- Benson, Sara R., ed. *Copyright Conversations: Rights Literacy in a Digital World.* Chicago: Association of College and Research Libraries, 2019.
- Coates, Jessica, Victoria Owen, and Susan Reilly, eds. *Navigating Copyright for Libraries: Purpose and Scope.* IFLA Publication, no. 149, 2021.
- Crews, Kenneth D. *Copyright Law for Librarians and Educators: Creative Strategies and Practical Solutions.* 4th ed. Chicago: American Library Association, 2020.
- Hirtle, Peter, Emily Hudson, and Andrew T. Kenyon. *Copyright and Cultural Institutions: Guidelines for Digitization for U.S. Libraries, Archives, and Museums.* Ithaca, NY: Cornell University Library, 2009. https://hdl.handle .net/1813/14142.
- Myers, Carla. *Copyright and Course Reserves: Legal Issues and Best Practices for Academic Libraries.* Santa Barbara: ABC-CLIO, 2021.
- Smith, Kevin L., and Erin L. Ellis, eds. *Coaching Copyright.* Chicago: American Library Association, 2019.

Index

f denotes figures; *t* denotes tables